C000051544

About the author

Matthew Benns is a journalist with *The Sun-Herald*. Before moving to Australia he worked in London for *The Daily Mail*, *Today* and *The Sun*, and also as a freelancer with articles appearing in *The Times*, *The Telegraph* and *The Guardian*. He now lives in Sydney.

When the Bough Breaks

The true story of child killer

Kathleen Folbigg

MATTHEW BENNS

BANTAM

SYDNEY • AUCKLAND • TORONTO • NEW YORK • LONDON

WHEN THE BOUGH BREAKS
A BANTAM BOOK

First published in Australia and New Zealand in 2003
by Bantam

Copyright © Matthew Benns, 2003

All rights reserved. No part of this publication may be reproduced,
stored in a retrieval system, transmitted in any form or by any means,
electronic, mechanical, photocopying, recording or otherwise, without
the prior written permission of the publisher.

National Library of Australia
Cataloguing-in-Publication Entry

  Benns, Matthew.
  When the bough breaks: the true story of child killer
  Kathleen Folbigg.

  ISBN: 1 86325 423 4

  1. Folbigg, Kathleen. 2. Filicide – Australia.
  3. Infanticide – Australia. 4. Women serial murderers – Australia.
  I. Title.

Transworld Publishers,
a division of Random House Australia Pty Ltd
20 Alfred Street, Milsons Point, NSW 2061
http://www.randomhouse.com.au

Random House New Zealand Limited
18 Poland Road, Glenfield, Auckland

Transworld Publishers,
a division of The Random House Group Ltd
61-63 Uxbridge Road, London W5 5SA

Random House Inc
1745 Broadway, New York, New York 10036

Cover photographs © News Limited and Corbis/APL
Cover and picture section design by Darian Causby/Highway 51
Typeset by Midland Typesetters, Maryborough, Victoria
Printed and bound by Griffin Press, Netley, South Australia

10 9 8 7 6 5 4 3 2

This book is dedicated to my father,
John Benns, and all the unsung heroes
who make sacrifices every day to see
their children safely into adulthood.

In memory of
Caleb, Patrick, Sarah and Laura Folbigg

Contents

Prologue

HER MOTHER'S GROWL of rage and frustration made 19-month-old Laura Folbigg drop to the kitchen floor in terror. She could not move. She was shaking and sobbing.

'I can't handle her when she's like this!' screamed Mummy.

If only Laura could get to Daddy. He had come running down the hall and was standing on the other side of the kitchen. Frozen to the spot as well. Mummy had been pinning Laura's arms down in the highchair and telling her to eat her breakfast. But she did not want to eat. She was not hungry. And that made Mummy mad.

Now Daddy was coming. He scooped her up in his arms and headed down the hall to the bedroom. She felt safe now. It was nice being cuddled by Daddy.

'Mummies and daddies argue but it doesn't mean they don't love you,' he cooed.

They were sitting on the bed. It felt safe. He smelled nice. But then Mummy came to the bedroom door.

'Give me that baby,' she demanded.

'Just fuck off,' replied Daddy.

'You give me that baby and get ready for work. Get out. You make her behave like this. This is your fault!' cried Mummy.

Ouch! Mummy grabbed hold of Laura's arm while Daddy still held her on his lap. He was upset and angry now too.

'Kath, just let her go. Just leave her. Piss off,' said Daddy. 'You look like you're going to punch some-body.'

'If I'm going to punch anybody it'll be you. Just give me that bloody baby,' snarled Mummy.

Daddy let go and Mummy carried her away.

Then Daddy left for work.

And Laura died.

1
Caleb

IN 1988 CRAIG AND KATHY Folbigg were happy. They had been married for a year, had their own small house in the Newcastle working-class suburb of Mayfield, and Craig had a good job as a car valuer. They both wanted to become parents and have a family. All they needed to make their lives complete was a baby.

Craig had first met Kathy Marlborough when she was in her late teens and working as a waitress at an Indian restaurant. She had left Kotara High School at the age of 15 to work at the checkout of a local service station. Friends from her high-school days recall a quiet, unremarkable student who had the usual circle of girlfriends.

Craig was a confident car fanatic, six years Kathy's senior. The first time he saw Kathy he thought she was sexy and sassy and he fell for her – hard. They went out together drinking, dancing and having fun. They dated through 1985, and in January 1986 Kathy moved in with Craig. After becoming engaged in August 1986, they bought their Mayfield house in

May 1987. Craig felt he had a home again for the first time since he was 15, at which time his mother had died of a cerebral haemorrhage, aged only 43. His father had later remarried but the death of his mother left Craig longing for a home of his own – a craving that was only satisfied when he met Kathy. He invested a deep love in her that may have blinded him to some of her shortcomings.

In August 1987 they were married. Kathy was 20; Craig was 25. Their wedding photograph shows a young couple full of love and hope. Kathy is beaming, her eyes fixed on Craig, her face alight with happiness. Her full-toothed smile is irrepressible. Craig is looking down at Kathy's ring, attempting to suppress a grin that suggests he feels like the cat that got the cream. It was probably one of the happiest days of Craig's life thus far.

In May 1988, the Folbiggs' wish for a baby was granted when Kathy fell pregnant. Craig and Kathy did all the things expectant parents enjoy: setting up the baby's bedroom together and buying things to welcome the new addition to their family.

Caleb Gibson Folbigg was born on 1 February 1989 at the Western Suburbs Maternity Hospital at Waratah in Newcastle. It was a long labour of nearly 18 hours and Kathy needed an epidural before the baby was finally delivered with forceps. The baby boy was fit and healthy. His Apgar score – which checks the baby's heartbeat, breathing, muscle tone, reflexes and colour one minute after birth and five minutes after birth – was good. Baby Caleb was taken and placed in a humidicrib for a few hours to recover from the birth and then reunited with his mother. Kathy was exhausted but happy. The epidural had caused her a few problems so she stayed in hospital with Caleb for five days. It took her a month to start walking comfortably again.

Craig found his wife happy to be a mum, although she was unwilling to breastfeed Caleb because she found it uncomfortable. Her distress and discomfort seemed to rub off on the baby. But after the nurses explained the benefits of breastfeeding to the new parents Kathy made another attempt to get Caleb to breastfeed.

There was one small problem with Caleb: he had great difficulty breathing through his nose. This made feeding difficult. He would drink, suck like crazy, then make a strange noise and have to break away to take a couple of breaths. Then he would start sucking again. This did not seem normal to his father but it was a problem that had been picked up while Kathy and Caleb were still in hospital and it had improved to the point where it was no longer distressing the baby by the time they were back at home.

As a result of the feeding problem, Kathy took Caleb to see a paediatrician at Royal Newcastle

Hospital, Dr Barry Springthorpe, to find out more about why he was having so much trouble feeding. She wanted to find out whether there was anything that could be done to make things easier for him.

Dr Springthorpe had been responsible for developing a Child Development Unit in Newcastle in 1976 to look at child development problems, Sudden Infant Death Syndrome (SIDS) and child abuse. He had also established a group called the Suspected Child Abuse and Neglect group (SCAN) to look into the problem of child abuse. He had practised in Yorkshire in the United Kingdom and at various places in Canada before moving to Newcastle. Drawing on all of his professional experience, he examined each of his patients for signs of abuse. He found no signs of any abuse when he examined two-week-old Caleb Folbigg on 17 February 1989 and took a photograph of the baby with his mother.

The news from the consultation with the paediatrician was reassuring. The doctor checked over the baby and found mild stridor – a sinking-in of the chest cage when breathing in. He thought this was due to laryngomalacia – a floppy larynx. Some children have softer than average cartilage, which can then collapse on inspiration, or breathing in. 'It is just noisy breathing, which is not apparent when the children are at rest, but if they exert themselves or cry, then the stridor becomes more apparent,' said

Dr Springthorpe. He asked if the mild breathing problem interfered with Caleb's feeding or sleeping and was informed by Kathy that it did not. He reassured Kathy that the condition would improve during infancy and that the vast majority of babies did not have the problem past 12 months of age.

Kathy took Caleb home and gave Craig the good news that their son was fine. It was a happy time for them both as they revelled in their role as the new parents of a gorgeous little baby, doing what all other new parents do, observing whose nose their baby had, whose fingers and so on. Caleb was well cared for, clean and tidy, and appeared to be thriving.

Two days after the appointment with Dr Springthorpe the Folbiggs took their new baby over to the home of Craig's brother, John, in Charlestown, Newcastle, to spend the day there. Craig had been working for most of Caleb's life so far – nearly three weeks – so it was a wonderful opportunity for him to see his wife and son together. To him, they seemed fine.

Caleb was well but by the end of the day was tired. By the time they drove home at 8pm he was fast asleep. Kathy changed him into a cloth nappy, singlet and yellow jumpsuit and gave him his 100ml of infant formula Infalac from a bottle, which he did not appear to have much trouble drinking. Kathy put him down in the bassinette in his bedroom – the front sunroom of the house. Both Craig and Kathy looked in on him before going to bed themselves a couple of hours later at 10.30pm. Sleeping peacefully, Caleb was wrapped in a bunny rug with a white baby blanket on top. The lamp was left on to make it easier for Kathy to feed him in the night.

The couple retired to the adjacent main bedroom, Kathy sleeping on the side of the bed nearest the door so that she could get up in the night without tripping over Craig or any clothes on the floor. Tired after their day out, they both went straight to sleep – Craig deeply. He had never tended to Caleb in the night because his son's cries never woke him. Once he closed his eyes, until they opened again in the morning he reckoned he wouldn't have known whether a truck had come through the wall or a bomb had fallen, he was such a sound sleeper. On the other hand, the baby's cries did wake Kathy, even though before he was born she could sleep for hours on end. She later described herself as one of those people who wouldn't see 10 o'clock twice in a day if they could help it. That had all changed with the birth of Caleb; she would wake up instantly as soon as he cried out and feed him on demand. With Caleb this meant a feed every three to four hours – each one lasting half an hour, because of his breathing difficulty. Kathy followed the routine for early-morning feeds she had started to establish where she tried not to turn the lights on, or stir up the baby too much once he had woken. She would sit with him in a chair in the lounge room in semi-darkness and feed and burp him, without saying a word. The baby would fall asleep and she would put him back to bed.

What was now about to happen would change their lives forever.

On this particular night, 20 February, with Craig fast asleep, only Kathy was able to later relate her version of what happened to Caleb after she had got up in the night to feed him. Caleb was asleep in her arms before she had risen from the chair. She burped him to try to bring some wind up, as she had been taught in hospital. As soon as he brought up some wind he fell asleep and she stood up from the lounge and walked into the bedroom to lay him down in his bassinette. 'We weren't told back then . . . to roll them over on their sides or any of that sort of business,' she said. 'When I left the room again he was sleepin' quite comfortable. So, yeah, I went back to bed. I went to the toilet and then went back to bed. I remember goin', I used to always go to the toilet after I had done it and then go back to bed.'

Kathy drifted back off to sleep; for how long she couldn't be sure. She stirred and decided to get up and check that everything was all right throughout the house, even though the baby was not crying for a feed.

Craig's and Kathy's recollections of what happened next varied. Craig thought they had left the bedside

light on; Kathy thought the street lamps outside illumi-
nated the room. She said: 'It wasn't pitch dark in the
room because the house is fairly close to the road, so
we had street lights. So, yeah, all I remember is that it
wasn't dark. I've sort of walked in there and been able
to semi see, I suppose, if you could call it that. Got to
the door, sort of looked around to check, which is all I
ever used to do. And if I could, usually you could hear,
you can hear babies breathing; they are very definite in
how they take a breath. So when I sort of didn't hear
that, that's when I thought, what have you done, have
you rolled over or something? Which is impossible,
three weeks old, but with your first child you don't
know. And I have just placed my hand on his chest and
didn't feel it sort of rise. And that's when I just threw the
light on and sort of rushed over to see why.

'I don't remember what exactly happened after that
because . . . it was just callin' out to Craig, which I had
to do three times because he's . . . he is a sound sleeper
and sort of doesn't react straight away . . . I think while
I'm yellin' I've sort of just thrown the covers off and
scooped him up and I have probably gone running into
the bedroom by the time I said the third "Craig!" and
it's just gone from there. I think he's gotten out of the
bed and we have both just sort of run, tryin', one of us
is going to the phone. And back then, unfortunately, we
didn't know about CPR . . . or any of that sort of thing.
So it was a case of both of us pretty much panicking on

what we were supposed to be doing . . . and we just rang the ambulance.'

Craig remembers being woken by a scream and jumping out of bed to find Kathy standing at the bassinette in Caleb's room screaming 'My baby, there's something wrong with my baby'. Contrary to Kathy's version of events, Craig recalled that Caleb was still in the bassinette, wrapped in the bunny rug. Grabbing him up out of the bassinette, Craig felt that his skin was warm but saw that his lips were blue and his eyes were closed. He put Caleb's face up to his ear but couldn't hear him breathing.

Craig was distraught. He didn't know much about CPR at the time, other than what he had seen on TV. Attempting to do what he thought was CPR he screamed at Kathy to call an ambulance. Kathy remembers being able to hear the sirens almost as soon as she had hung up the phone from her 000 call. Meanwhile, Craig was frantically trying to save his son. He had him laid out on the lounge and was blowing into his mouth. He continued his efforts until relieved by an ambulance officer 10 minutes later.

Kathy later recalled the ambulance arriving: 'We already had the door open, I think, no I can't remember whether I had Caleb or Craig had Caleb, it's all just . . .

'From once I actually found him and realised that something wasn't actually quite right and once I've flung a light on it's all just, just a blur. There's only sort of bits and pieces that stick in my mind after that.'

Ambulance officers David Hopkins and Richard Baines arrived at the house one minute before 3am on 20 February 1989 to find Craig and Kathy weeping beside the body of their 19-day-old baby. Officer Hopkins removed Caleb's upper clothing and established that he was in a state of cardiac arrest – unconscious, not breathing and pulseless. He noted that the baby was still warm to the touch but pale around the mouth and lips. His partner, Officer Baines, cleared the baby's airways. Observing how upset the couple was, the ambulance officers asked Craig to take Kathy into the bedroom while they worked on resuscitating Caleb.

Officer Baines cleared Caleb's mouth of fluid and inserted a Guedel's airway, a curved plastic tube into the back of Caleb's mouth to hold back his tongue. They desperately attempted to revive the baby using mouth-to-mouth resuscitation and external cardiac massage. Other ambulance officers arrived and assisted with electrocardiograph tracing. It was to no avail. Thirty-nine minutes after arriving, the officers informed Kathy and Craig that their son was dead.

In his report Officer Hopkins wrote what he felt was an appropriate provisional diagnosis based on the history he had elicited from the parents and also on his previous experience of such cases: 'Sudden Infant

Death Syndrome'. This was certainly an educated judgment. However, Kathy's record of the event had a different tone. As part of her way of caring for Caleb, Kathy had kept a diary for the 19 days he was alive. She made entries almost every half-hour as she monitored his progress. Craig saw her regular use of the black A4 diary as a new mum's way of coping. The final entry for Caleb's life at 2am on Sunday 20 February read: 'Finally asleep!!'

Later that morning a police officer from Mayfield arrived at the house. Craig later recalled that he did not ask the Folbiggs much at all about the tragic events of the night but came to extend his sympathies. Craig then accompanied the officer to the hospital in Newcastle to formally identify Caleb.

Craig was inconsolable. What had gone wrong? How could their beautiful baby son have died?

Later on the same day at the hospital, he and Kathy were introduced to a representative from the SIDS organisation who ran a parents' retreat in Charlestown. She was very kind and supportive. Gently she explained to them that children could die suddenly and unexpectedly and when no obvious cause of death was found then it was attributed to SIDS. In the late 1980s there was not a lot known about SIDS. It was a mystery. Craig and Kathy would have to come to terms with the horrible fact that for a reason nobody could understand their son had just stopped breathing.

The SIDS counsellor told them they could try to have another baby. It seldom happened again.

This was of little comfort to the Folbiggs as they drove home that day and returned to an empty house and a hollow life. Craig sat down to telephone the same family and friends he had called with such delight less than three weeks before to announce Caleb's birth. Now he had to go through the same phone list again and tell his and Kathy's loved-ones that little Caleb was dead.

The next morning Kathy called Dr Springthorpe to inform him that Caleb had died. He contacted Dr Roy Cummings who conducted the post-mortem on Caleb. The cause of death was not able to be established but Dr Springthorpe was specifically concerned about the baby's larynx and asked Dr Cummings to particularly check whether there were any cysts or webs that cause noisy breathing if they occur. No evidence was found of these and the doctors concluded the stridor, or floppy larynx, was not the cause of Caleb's death. This remained a mystery. It was officially recorded as Sudden Infant Death Syndrome.

Concerned for the grieving parents, Dr Springthorpe made an appointment for Kathy and Craig to come in and see him. He noted that the family had been counselled and that Craig was very bitter but seemed to be coping. He explained the finding of SIDS to them. 'We look for a possible cause and, if we are unable to establish that cause, then it is put in the broad category of sudden infant death. It should really be called sudden unexpected death in infancy, or sudden unexplained death in infancy.'

Craig was devastated. As the weeks went by, he continued to mourn for his son. Kathy, on the other hand, appeared to be coping much better. While Craig felt that he was falling to pieces he noticed his wife was not affected in the same way – she basically just got on with her life and returned to work at the restaurant she was employed at before Caleb's birth. Craig sat at home and grieved; she went out to friends' houses and to nightclubs.

While grieving alone, in his mind Craig replayed the months leading up to the birth of Caleb and the 19 days of his short life. Something was nagging at him. Not the way Kathy had treated Caleb so much as her disposition as a mother. She seemed to have resented not being the same centre of attention she had been in pregnancy, once the child was born. And from that time on he wondered why he never really got to spend any time around his sisters after they gave birth to their children other than to pay a quick visit to see the babies. Why did Kathy not like to be around their children? It was a doubt he would lock away in his heart and not voice for 14 years after Caleb had been laid to rest.

2

Patrick

IT TOOK A LONG TIME for Craig to raise himself from the black hole of despair that Caleb's death had created. When he did manage to lift his head, it was to find Kathy was already living their former, more carefree life. Slowly, as he rejoined the world, one thought remained with him. What he wanted, more than anything else, was to be a dad. Craig and Kathy began to talk about having another baby.

At the prospect of having more children, the couple was guided by the current advice about SIDS prevention. Studies had shown that there were links between the socio-economic status and incidences of SIDS. Essentially, more cot deaths seemed to occur in poorer households. The SIDS organisations that Craig and Kathy were in contact with advised them on what they assumed was a common scenario for SIDS babies in terms of low-income demographics, type of housing and environmental factors. The Folbiggs took this information on board and set about renovating their old, draughty house. They recarpeted, painted and had new blinds put up. The sunroom where Caleb had slept had been fairly rundown and small with a door that opened onto the driveway. Craig and his father bricked up that door and installed a big window in the room, and improved the internals as well.

Craig and Kathy were also advised that there was a link between smoking and cot death. That was one thing Craig could rule out as the cause of Caleb's death. Kathy had never been a big smoker; she might have had the odd puff in her life, but that was about it. Craig had been a smoker for most of his life but after he and Kathy had bought their house at Mayfield and Kathy had fallen pregnant with Caleb, she had asked Craig not to smoke in the house because she didn't like it. Craig obliged and never smoked in the house again, and certainly never smoked around the baby in a confined space.

With the renovations underway and with smoking ruled out as a contributing factor to Caleb's death, Craig was eager to have another child. It was not long before Kathy fell pregnant, although she later recalled that the pregnancy was more of a happy mistake than a planned pregnancy, and that they had been doing the renovations more to occupy themselves than in anticipation of an imminent pregnancy. While the couple renovated the house properly they lived in a caravan in the backyard. By the time Kathy was ready to give birth the house was ready and the danger areas identified by the SIDS experts had been removed.

On the morning of 3 June 1990 Kathy went into labour. Craig had already left for work. She had some bad Braxton Hicks – false contractions – before Craig left for the day but she felt he had not taken her very seriously. When he was leaving for work he joked, 'When you have a real one, call me.'

Just after he left Kathy recognised that the contractions were definitely real but could not contact him because he was driving to work. Instead she had to turn to Craig's brother Greg who lived just around the corner. He turned up minutes later in his Volvo and drove her to the Western Suburbs Hospital in Newcastle. Once they had arrived, Craig's brother called him at work from the maternity ward to let him know Kathy was in labour. 'Now you can come and see her; she's having real ones.'

This time Kathy did not need drugs or forceps and the labour was much quicker than with Caleb. Craig arrived in time for the birth and was present when Patrick Allen David Folbigg was delivered.

The first thing his parents noticed was their son's blond hair and blue eyes and how much he resembled Craig. They were also pleased with his brilliant Apgar score. Craig was euphoric and although she also appeared ecstatic to her husband, a bit later Kathy wrote in her diary:

This was the day that Patrick Allen David Folbigg was born. I had mixed feelings this day whether or not I was going to cope as a mother and whether I was going to get stressed out like I did last time. I often regret Caleb and Patrick only because your life changes so much and maybe I'm not a person who likes change, but we will see.

Once again Kathy did not like breastfeeding the baby. As she felt a little insecure with new baby Patrick she stayed in hospital for five days even though there were no obvious problems. She went through the whole process of learning how to bath and look after babies all over again.

This time, Craig was more involved. He was scared he might lose Patrick, and felt nervous knowing that SIDS was still a mystery. Because he had not really spent much time with Caleb at all, he quit his job so that he could stay at home with Patrick and Kathy.

As far as Craig was concerned, Patrick was 'a great little bloke'. He fed and slept well and was perfectly healthy. As with Caleb, Craig was the only member of the family who was sleeping through the night. Kathy was feeding Patrick every few hours in the lounge room or in his bedroom. Patrick was not sleeping in his brother's room but in a renovated bedroom off the dining room towards the rear of the house. Kathy and Craig felt it was the most secure, protected and least draughty room of the house, even though it was further away from their bedroom than the sunroom. Not that there was any trouble hearing the baby. Little Patrick Folbigg knew his place in the world and would let everyone know when it was his dinnertime. As soon as he cried, everybody knew about it.

Patrick had none of the breathing problems his brother suffered. Kathy was pleased with his progress. In his first couple of months he would wake up in the early hours, around three or four o'clock, the same way Caleb had done. By the time he was almost three months old he was only waking up once during the night and was already in a routine where he was quite happily fed and back in bed at about midnight or one o'clock in the morning, not waking up again until around 6am. He had no problems with his health and was thriving.

During his time at home, Craig thought his wife was coping wonderfully with motherhood. In his eyes, she seemed to enjoy being a mum and did not appear to be having any difficulties with it. The family was secure; they owned their own home and car and had no debts, except for their recent renovations. Life was going really well. In fact, things were going so well that Craig considered going back to work when Newcastle's Holden dealer sought him out to be the workshop controller. It was a good job and Craig figured he couldn't stay home forever. He accepted the job.

Big mistake.

On Wednesday 17 October 1990 Craig came home from the third day in his new job to what appeared to be a normal family. Kathy dressed Patrick in a nappy, pilchers, singlet and pyjamas and tucked him into bed at 8.30pm. Two hours later Craig went into the baby's bedroom and kissed Patrick goodnight. The lamp was on and Patrick was sleeping contentedly on his back.

Kathy later said that she had done the midnight or one o'clock feed without incident and had returned to bed when she again inexplicably woke up. 'Again it was a case of me finding myself awake for some reason or other and I have gotten up and thought, well, I need to go to the toilet, I'll go now and I'll check him on the way past 'cause I had to go past to go to the toilet. So when I stopped at the door to check on him – because again I have placed his bed that he was sleeping in across from the door so easy access – I sort of was listening for his breathing and noticed that it was laboured; it was as if he was trying very hard to draw a breath . . . so I have just immediately flung on a light and we've gone into action from there.'

Craig was woken by Kathy's bloodcurdling scream and ran down to Patrick's room. Because it was a little room, the cot was positioned behind the door so when he ran through the door he had to slam it after him to get to the cot. Kathy was standing at the end of the cot screaming.

The side of the wooden cot was still up. Patrick was lying on his back with the covers down near the bottom of the mattress. His eyes were closed and he looked as if he were asleep. Kathy was still at the end of the cot screaming. No words – just hysterical noise. Craig grabbed his son and screamed at Kathy to phone an ambulance. Cradling Patrick in his arms he heard a small noise coming from the baby. 'Oh God, he's breathing,' thought Craig. The baby was still warm and his skin was pink. Craig put him on the floor and started to try to do CPR on him, placing his mouth over Patrick's mouth and nose in the way he had been shown by the SIDS advisers. Unfortunately though, Craig still had not undertaken any proper CPR training.

Once again, Kathy could not remember whether she or Craig rang the ambulance. Craig, however, has photographic recall of the event and as he performed CPR on Patrick on the bedroom floor, he remembers Kathy on the phone explaining to the ambulance service where they were.

Ambulance officer David Hopkins had no trouble finding his way from Hamilton Ambulance Station to 36 Rawson Street Mayfield that morning. He had been one of the two ambulance officers who had rushed to the same address the year before to try to save baby Caleb.

At 4.41am on Thursday 18 October 1990, Officer Hopkins, with another ambulance officer in tow, arrived to be greeted by a similar scene to the one that had met him in 1989. 'My baby is having trouble breathing and won't wake up properly!' Kathy cried.

The officer took Baby Patrick, removed the clothes from the upper part of his body, and immediately noticed that he was pale around the face and struggling to breathe. Very listless and with a decreased level of consciousness, the baby was in respiratory distress. Patrick was desperately using all the muscles in his abdomen and the intercostal muscles between his ribs in his battle to get air into his little lungs.

Hopkins noticed a tracheal tug – where the pressure of inspiration pulls the skin and soft tissue at the neck – when Patrick breathed inwards. He noticed that upon inspiration the baby's ribs extended out further than they normally would. Poor Patrick was fighting for his life.

The ambulance officers sat Patrick on Kathy's lap on the stretcher and administered oxygen therapy en route to the hospital. What stuck in Kathy's mind was that as soon as Patrick was given oxygen his eyes shot open, even though he was still obviously having difficulty breathing. The oxygen therapy appeared to be working as Patrick's consciousness rose, even though he was still struggling to breathe.

By 4.52am the ambulance had conveyed Patrick and his parents to the Mater Hospital in Newcastle. Emergency staff in the hospital's casualty section sprang into action. Doctors and nurses came from every direction to work on Patrick and attach him to a tangle of cords and beeping monitors.

Dr Joseph Dezordi was working as the hospital resident paediatrics night doctor when the ambulance crew burst through the doors of casualty with Kathy and Patrick on a stretcher. 'I was called to emergency before sunrise,' Dr Dezordi later recalled. 'Patrick was brought in by ambulance . . . and he was classified as an emergency with problems of cyanosis; that is, he was blue, not pink . . . There was a history that he had been coughing beforehand at home. When I saw the baby he was lethargic and not active.'

He noted that Patrick did not have a fever and did not respond to even quite painful stimuli. The doctor swung into rapid action. He took a brief description of what had happened from Kathy and then organised oxygen for Patrick and took a blood sample to try to establish what was wrong with him. Patrick appeared to be improving. He was pink and the blood test showed he had oxygen in his bloodstream.

It was close to dawn and Craig was standing near the bed where the medical team was working on his son when all of a sudden the baby's eyes shot open again, just as they had done briefly in the ambulance. As Patrick stabilised his father felt a flash of hope. To Craig, Patrick seemed groggy, like he had been through hell, but he seemed fine.

Kathy recalled later: 'By the time we got to the hospital . . . family members and that had been called . . . so I'm assuming Craig had called them . . . The oxygen was on him [Patrick]. I can't remember if they were giving him injections of anything to try and get him to respond to anything in particular, but it was just like switching on a light switch. One minute he was laying on the bed in the hospital not being responsive and just sort of with the oxygen mask and the next minute it was like bang, he was just awake and screaming and panicking because all these people were there . . . It even took me ages and ages to . . . get him to calm down 'cause it was like, I don't know whether it was like he must have been in some sort of deep sleep state and all of a sudden . . . there's bright lights and there's people with white coats hanging around and things on him and things on his chest and he just sort of freaked.'

Dr Dezordi organised a chest X-ray, which came back as normal. He noted that Patrick's development appeared normal for a four-month-old baby and examined his airways to try to find a blockage that could have obstructed his airways and caused the baby to gasp for life as he had. There was no evidence of croup or any food or milk that Patrick could have choked on.

Further tests were carried out. Serious illnesses such as meningitis, septicaemia or bacterial infection were ruled out by the tests. However, the test results did reveal one unexpected finding – a high level of glucose in Patrick's urine. Dr Dezordi found this result to be of interest because babies, and even adults for that matter, do not have glucose in their urine normally, unless they are diabetics. Baby Patrick was not diabetic. Dr Dezordi acknowledged later that the existence of a large amount of glucose in the urine suggested a fairly catastrophic event, anything that stopped the air getting into Patrick's lungs and reduced the oxygen levels in his blood and brain, such as an asphyxiating event or a prolonged seizure. That this might have been caused by something other than a seizure was not the uppermost thought in the busy doctor's mind.

Patrick's first CAT scan upon arrival at the hospital could only have given his parents hope. His brain was normal. However, as the hours wore on the damage that had occurred to his brain became increasingly apparent.

As his condition stabilised Patrick was moved up to the children's ward. The next night, Friday, Craig was nursing him when all of a sudden the baby stiffened in his arms. His eyes rolled back and he started to shake. Craig did not know what a fit was but he knew something was very wrong with his baby. The medical staff tended to Patrick straight away and recognised that he was having a seizure. Life for the Folbigg family was about to get very difficult indeed.

Paediatric neurologist Dr Ian Wilkinson was assigned to care for Patrick and instigated a number of tests, particularly an electroencephalogram to measure the electrical functioning of his brain. This showed the baby's condition was deteriorating as time wore on. Dr Wilkinson noted that Patrick seemed very subdued when he had first seen him. The doctor was concerned at that stage that there may have been a primary problem within his brain. Patrick subsequently developed seizures and convulsions around the third day of his admission to the hospital. His brain was effectively short-circuiting.

Dr Wilkinson was aware that Patrick had a sibling who had already died, so had considered the possibility that there could be some type of health disorder in the family that had produced abnormalities within both Caleb and Patrick. With this in mind, an extremely exhaustive system of testing was carried out on Patrick – all the available tests at the disposal of the doctors at the time. Blood was sent to the Adelaide Children's Hospital and overseas for testing to check whether there were any chemical deficiencies in the brain. A rectal biopsy was sent to the Prince of Wales Hospital in Sydney to see if there were any abnormalities in the nerves. White blood cells were stained for a similar test. Absolutely no inherited diseases that might have brought about neurological abnormalities were found. According to the doctor, Patrick's condition was entirely consistent with him suffering a catastrophic asphyxiating event from unknown causes.

'It's a very typical sort of story that a child, who's suffered some asphyxial damage to the brain may then, over the next few days and weeks, develop progressive change within the brain that produces seizures. So, it is quite common that . . . the child . . . may not have seizures initially. It's quite common to find that further down the road they may have seizures.

'I mean there is a lot of swelling that goes on in the brain as a consequence of asphyxia. That may not reach its maximum until the second, third or fourth day. Also we know that scarring can occur as a result of lack of oxygen – what we call gliosis – and the development of that scarring may result in an irritation of the normal electrical activity of the brain and then produce seizures, but it is not uncommon to find that there is a gap, really, between the event and then the development of seizures.'

Essentially a healthy four-month-old had suffered an asphyxial event so terrible that he was now an epileptic and was being given the powerful barbiturate phenobarbitone to control his seizures. After a battery of further tests and scans Patrick was discharged from hospital on 29 October 1990. Dr Dezordi filled out his five-page discharge summary with the suggestion that Patrick was suffering 'intractable seizures, probably viral encephalitis'. That possibility was loosely voiced as a possible cause after discussion with the many doctors who had seen Patrick during his time in hospital. Dr Dezordi never believed he had encephalitis, a viral inflammation of the brain, because none of the tests or lumbar punctures pointed to that. None of the tests had shown a medical reason for his dramatic decline. Dr Dezordi could find no medical cause for Patrick's illness. To all the doctors who treated him, the cause of Patrick's condition was a complete mystery. When he was sent home from the hospital with his mother, the mystery remained unsolved.

3
Patrick's Twilight

CRAIG FOLBIGG WILL NEVER forget his 29th birthday on 21 November 1990. It was the day he was told by doctors that his baby son was blind, just as he and Kathy were getting ready to take him home from yet another of their seemingly endless return trips to consult with specialists and doctors at the hospital. The hope that had blossomed from Patrick's recovery on the night of his attack turned out to be false and there had been nothing but bad news ever since.

Kathy and Craig were in shock. They wondered whether he was suffering from total blindness because they had felt that he had been looking at them when they tried to talk to him, but then the next minute they'd look at their son and he'd seem to be staring through or past them. They took him to different specialists to try to figure out how blind he was.

The specialists explained Patrick's limitations. If something was held in front of him and kept stationary he would be able to focus and see it but as soon as the object was moved even slightly he seemed to lose perception. Kathy explained later: 'That took us a bit of getting used to because we sort of had to realise that when speaking to him you had to sort of keep him stationary and you had to keep your face pretty much in front of him.'

Dr Wilkinson believed that Patrick's blindness stemmed directly from the time he suffered that catastrophic asphyxiating event. It became apparent to him, further down the line, that Patrick had lost visual function. He had seen the same thing in a number of situations where children suffered various asphyxial events and subsequently developed visual problems. He believed that it was because the visual part of the brain is extraordinarily sensitive to lack of oxygen. 'It is one part of the brain that, following oxygen deprivation, may show malfunction – perhaps even in an isolated fashion.'

The localised damage to the occipital lobes, the back part of the brain, also explained the seizures that had Craig and Kathy making seemingly endless trips to the hospital with their son in the weeks before Christmas that year. Kathy saw the seizures as a 'sneaky kind' of epilepsy – it was not the type of epilepsy where the body would jerk and physically shake; rather his eyes would just roll into the back of his head while he was lying down. Kathy felt it was as if Patrick was looking up at the top of his brain for some reason. He would stay like that for anything from a few seconds to a minute or more.

This made life very difficult for the Folbiggs. Craig knew that his wife had a huge burden to bear with all the extra work Patrick's condition involved. On top of what he considered 'all the normal mum stuff' – feeding him, bathing him, teaching him things – she had to deal with his medication and keep up with all the advice from the Royal Blind Society, so as to make sure he was developing at an acceptable rate compared to other children of his age. She had to follow advice from physiotherapists to try to teach Patrick how to crawl and how to develop other age-appropriate motor skills and activities. Kathy later said: 'We had to try and teach him how to feed and drink and do all the rest of it, knowing that he sort of couldn't see and do all that sort of thing. It was hard work but Craig and I were just so relieved that he had survived.'

Kathy also recalled later that at the time she felt she was on autopilot, trying to tell herself that the important thing was that Patrick had survived and that it was not really an issue to either Craig or her if they had to struggle through these hard times so that Patrick continued to survive. Craig, however, felt his wife was not coping very well with the added pressure. Every day Kathy would clench her fists in front of her and shake them as she growled in frustration. She was losing her temper with both him and the baby.

All of this put enormous strain on the relationship

between Kathy and Craig. Kathy felt that 99 per cent of her time was spent caring for Patrick. At that time even she realised that Craig came behind their pets in terms of priority and the level of care he received from her. She later said: 'He is the sort of man that requires someone to devote most of their time to him . . . I mean he could stand on his own two feet, I'm sure, but he does like someone to care and appreciate and all the rest of it. And his ego needs a slight inflation every now and then or he gets a bit depressed with himself . . . He required looking after and at that particular time I wasn't. I had a more important person on my mind.'

One fortunate thing was that the Folbiggs had a lot of family support. To alleviate some of her stress and to give herself time to do other things, Kathy was dropping off Patrick with Craig's sister Carol Newitt who lived close by. Carol had been somewhat of a substitute mother to Craig ever since their mother had died. She was also a nurse and lived with her husband and four older children just a five-minute drive away from Kathy and Craig. She was the natural person for them to turn to in their time of need.

Carol thought that Kathy was having trouble facing the inevitable future of life with a handicapped child and indeed Kathy had confided in her that she was having difficulty coping. One particular day, Kathy walked into Carol's house and handed over Patrick to her. 'You look after him. He is good for you and I can't get him to shut up,' she had said in frustration. Kathy was right; the baby *was* good for her sister-in-law. Carol loved little Patrick more than anything and thought he was an angel. On many occasions she helped Kathy with the physiotherapy required for Patrick to learn to crawl and sit up. She also helped to teach him to respond to noises so that he could reach for things. She would babysit for Craig and Kathy so they could go out and forget about their problems for a little while. And she was there during the extremely emotionally draining times when the baby had to be held safely as he experienced his fits.

Craig was at his wits' end over Kathy's diminishing ability to cope. She was withdrawn and was not talking to him. He needed to know how she really felt and in his desperation he went to her bedside table and took out the diary he had seen Kathy writing in at night. What he read shocked and upset him. In one entry Kathy had written that she wasn't coping, that it was all too much drama. She felt that her husband and son would be better off without her; that Craig could bring up Patrick with his family much better than she could. She wrote that she was going to work out a way to leave Craig with Patrick.

Once again Craig turned to his sister Carol for help. She came over to their house so that Craig and Kathy could talk through their situation and feelings with her. Kathy repeated what she had written in her diary – that she didn't think that she could stay with Craig and look after Patrick. She thought they would be better off if she left. Carol and Craig counselled Kathy, telling her that although they loved the baby very much and could look after him if she left, it was she who would always truly be Patrick's mother and would surely miss him if she left. Carol offered to look after Patrick more often and give further support to Kathy. Carol's words appeared to reassure Kathy and the crisis seemed to pass.

Patrick's general practitioner, Dr Christopher Marley, observed that he was a normal, healthy baby in all respects other than his epilepsy and sight problems. He had had some bad episodes over Christmas and New Year but he appeared to be getting better. He was progressing and growing well, and had fewer viral infections than most children his age, with no need for antibiotics to treat them. His mother acknowledged that he was a very determined baby – a good kid, happy and smiling 90 per cent of the time. Patrick seemed to do his best to make life easy for his mother with his very even temperament.

But even that did not save him.

On 13 February 1991 the Folbigg family got up at 6am and began their daily routine. Patrick was eight months old and now drinking cow's milk from a bottle and eating solids. Kathy got him up out of bed and he tucked into some toast at the dining table while Craig sat with him and had a cup of coffee. Craig insisted on having breakfast with his son even though Kathy would have preferred the routine to commence a little later. At 7.30am Craig picked up his son and kissed him. 'Who loves you, bubby?' he said, before handing him to Kathy at the door and heading off for work. It was a completely normal day.

Years later, Kathy recounted the events of the morning: 'We did the bath routine . . . and got changed for the day. It was the usual doing the washing and trying to clean up the house and whatever. He used to always be with me; whenever I was doing something he would be with me. I never let him out of my sight for any particular reason.'

By now Patrick was sleeping in Caleb's old room at the front of the house – the sunroom renovated by Craig and his father. Rooms and furniture changed regularly as Kathy moved things around and fine-tuned the house. 'He used to have a bit of a morning nap. Usually half an hour if I was lucky or an hour if he was really tired,' said Kathy, who could not remember exactly what time she put Patrick down that day. 'I would wait to hang all the washing out till he was in bed so as that I knew . . . I could go out the back . . . Somewhere where he was confined so that I didn't have to sort of worry about that.'

From this point, Kathleen Folbigg's mind becomes a complete blank. Years later she cried as she spoke about this mental block: 'With Patrick it's the whole day, the whole death, the whole sort of thing I have pretty much . . . just blocked it . . . probably because he was so sick and all the battle that we went through trying to keep him with us . . .'

What she did claim to remember years later was that she walked back into Patrick's bedroom. 'Whether it was a case of seeing if he was all right or just walking into the room to put washing away . . . I have walked in the room . . . and he was flat on his back which made me look twice because I used to always lay him on his sides and he used to stay there. He was a heavy sleeper, same as his dad, so he would sort of stay in sort of whatever position he was in when you put him to sleep. He was flat on his back so that made me look twice and he was pale again and my first thought . . . was "not another fit", because we hadn't had any for a while and we seemed to be going okay. So I thought, no, not another fit, but, yeah, it wasn't that, it was a case of he actually sort of wasn't breathing.'

It was around 10am that Carol Newitt's telephone rang. Kathy told her that it had happened again. Immediately Carol got into her car and drove over. Walking into the house she found Kathy sitting on the lounge with her elbows on her knees and her head down, crying, waiting for the ambulance and for Craig. Carol walked into Patrick's bedroom where he was lying as if he were asleep, with his little hands alongside his face, just as he had looked on numerous other occasions when Carol had put him down to sleep. The side of the cot was up but no bedclothes were covering him. Carol went to pick him up.

'No, don't. Don't pick him up,' cried Kathy.

It then really hit Carol that Patrick was dead. She just stood there, stroking his face, talking to him, imploring him to come back to them.

Meanwhile, Craig had been at work. At morning teatime he was making a cup of coffee for a workmate when he was informed by one of the girls he worked with that he was wanted on the phone. Walking over to his desk and picking up the phone he could hear Kathy screaming down the phone. 'It's happened again!'

'What's happened again? A fit or something?' demanded Craig.

'I need you. Come home.'

'Have you rung the ambulance?'

'Yes, yes, I have rung the ambulance.'

'I'm coming straight home,' cried Craig, before running for his car.

It was a harrowing five-minute drive for Craig, who took the shortest route home. As he rounded the corner of his street, he could see an ambulance speeding up from the other end. Craig drove straight up into his front yard and bolted from the car straight into the house and into Patrick's bedroom. There he found the baby still lying on his back in the cot, and his sister and wife in shock. Immediately Craig scooped up Patrick into his arms. The baby was still floppy and warm but his lips were blue so Craig put him on the lounge and tried in vain to revive him.

As Craig began blowing into his son's mouth and nose the ambulance crew came running into the house. Ambulance officer Murray Hetherington together with two of his colleagues from Toronto Ambulance Station had received the call at 10.02am. When they arrived, Patrick was not breathing. He was rushed into the ambulance accompanied by his two distraught parents and taken to the Mater Hospital in Waratah.

Of that stage in the emergency Kathy later claimed: 'I was still hopeful that . . . it wasn't another, you know . . . Caleb thing happening again.'

Patrick's specialist, Dr Wilkinson, who examined the baby, met them at the Mater in the casualty department. He found the baby to be unresponsive. Little Patrick had no spontaneous breathing; he had no cardiac beat at all and appeared pale and lifeless. Dr Wilkinson could see that Patrick was dead. His body was still warm, which seemed to indicate that his death was a fairly recent occurrence. The doctor broke the news to Craig and Kathy that it was futile to continue with the attempts to resuscitate their son. They could see that the doctor was right.

Dr Wilkinson filled out the death certificate stating that Patrick had died from asphyxia – suffocation – caused by an epileptic fit that he had not overcome. Later knowledge would cause Dr Wilkinson to revise that opinion.

Craig was unhappy with this opinion from the outset. He later said: 'We got him back after the Christmas episodes and he had been going really, really well. Hadn't missed a beat. He was on his Tegretol and stuff like that and he was going really well and he was a great little kid. He had so much courage it wasn't funny and it didn't matter what sort of came on him or what he had to put up with . . .'

Craig and Kathy's family came to the hospital to comfort the grief-stricken parents. Kathy's foster mother, Deirdre Marlborough, put her arms round Kathy, gently consoling her. She then attempted to hug Craig but he pushed his mother-in-law away. Distraught and beyond consolation, he was already withdrawing into himself in his grief.

On the day of his death a post-mortem was carried out on Patrick at the hospital by Dr Gurpreet Singh-Khaira under the supervision of his department head Dr Jan Bishop. They found he had been a well-nourished baby. His airways were clear. The brain did contain scarring from some kind of a hypoxic event in the past but they could find no apparent cause of death.

Slides containing tissue sections from Patrick's brain were sent to Dr Alex Kan at the Royal Alexandra Hospital for Children at Camperdown together with Dr Singh-Khaira's autopsy report. He concluded that the brain damage Patrick had suffered was caused by a lack of oxygen reaching the brain during an episode five months previously. Again the confusion about encephalitis being a possible cause clouded the issue, although the signs of Patrick having suffered it were by no means proven to Dr Kan.

The reports ended up on the desk of Patrick's specialist Dr Wilkinson. Years later, and with the benefit of hindsight, he viewed them differently but in 1991 the cause of death officially stated that Patrick had suffocated as a result of an epileptic seizure. Kathy and Craig were left to try to piece their life together again. One was much more successful at this than the other.

Craig was devastated by his son's death and at first thought his wife felt the same way. It quickly became apparent that they were grieving very differently. Shortly after Patrick's death he asked Kathy what had happened on that fateful morning. She told him that she had just gone into Patrick's bedroom to check on him 'and found him how he was and the rest [Craig] knew'. Kathy had a way of cutting off conversations to prevent further discussion. She claimed to have blanked the details from her own mind. The couple did not really talk any further about what had happened to their son.

Years later Craig described how he had been feeling at this time: 'I like to talk about things and I like to talk about Pat and Caleb and how they were as bubbies and how much fun they were and how loving they were . . . and how much fun it was being their dad. I tried . . . many, many times to coax Kathy into conversations like that and she would not talk about those babies. So, what you do to defend yourself from the inevitable of the fact that this girl wouldn't talk about the life that you had had, you just go into yourself.'

As Craig withdrew, Kathy went out. Ironically, three to four months after Patrick's funeral, Kathy started a job at BabyCo at Kotara. Craig found that she was back to what he described as her 'happy-go-lucky' self. He, meanwhile, was still grieving. As he tried to reconcile himself to life without his son a black despair cost him his job. He later explained: 'The world pretty much stopped for me. I lost my job. Didn't really see any sort of sunshine in any situation or anything like that and sort of went into myself, spent a lot of time in my garage, pretty much kept away from a lot of people, and that's how I am, and Kath just gets on with things. I wouldn't say that she just forgot the little fellow, but we packed all his stuff away, changed the room, just tried to get on with life. We had a neighbour that had a little fellow, Simon, and I used to go and steal Simon.'

Years later, the Folbiggs' neighbour and father of little Simon, Mark Lockley, spoke of this time: 'Craig thought the world of my young bloke and my young bloke calls him Uncle Craig. They got on like a house on fire.'

While the neighbours spent a great deal of time with Craig, they saw very little of Kathy. 'I certainly know that Craig was deeply affected by the death. It did not seem to upset her as much as it did Craig,' said Mark.

The couple rowed about their different forms of grief. Kathy wanted to go out, have fun and enjoy life. Craig felt he was in a type of personal hell. Describing this time years later he said: 'She would rip into me because all I wanted to do was dig a big black hole and bury myself in it – not get on with life, face the world, do anything. Pretty much that's what I got told.' So Craig resigned himself to going out with his wife as she socialised with friends and danced at nightclubs so that he could at least be with her.

Kathy no longer wanted to live in a house that had so many tragic memories. As part of an effort to leave the past behind the Folbiggs moved into a new house they bought at Dower Close in Thornton, near Maitland in the Hunter Valley.

As the couple tried to get on with life and Craig started working again Kathy dropped a bombshell. She told Craig she wanted another baby.

4

Sarah

'I NEVER WANT TO hear you scream like that again,' Craig Folbigg told his wife. 'I never want to see a dead baby again. I don't want to experience that pain again, the pain of losing a baby.' He was adamant. Craig simply could not face the thought of having another child.

Kathy told him she was prepared to risk that pain again and that having another child would be a leap of faith. It was, in reality, an ultimatum; she was telling Craig to give her another child and the chance to be a normal mother or else lose her.

Kathy persisted. Craig still had an overriding desire to be a dad but he had so many questions and concerns that he knew they needed to discuss. After Caleb and Patrick, could he risk going through it again? Was it right to chance another baby's life and their own happiness? Would this baby die like the others? Why had the other two died? Were there medical issues that needed to be checked? Should they accept that they should have no more children? Craig needed time to think and asked for space to think about it.

Kathy gave him a week. During this time she recruited his sister Carol to try to persuade Craig that having another child was a good idea. They talked it through over those seven days and eventually he relented and agreed they would try for another baby on one condition – they get the Sudden Infant Death Syndrome experts involved once the baby was born. Kathy felt no hesitation in agreeing to that; she knew that the main risk to the baby would not be SIDS.

Once Craig had made the decision to try for another child with Kathy he felt happy and anticipated how much fun it would be to be a dad again. With the decision made it did not take long for them to conceive. A year after Patrick died Kathy told her husband that she was pregnant. Once again, the couple was happy together and Craig felt their lives now had a direction. As they prepared for the arrival of their third child at their new home in the friendly cul-de-sac of Dower Place in Thornton they were reassured by the SIDS experts who were assisting them that, in keeping with the contemporary theory on SIDS, they would be offered a sleep-apnoea monitor once their baby was born. This helped remove some of the anxiety Craig felt about becoming a father again.

The birth of Sarah Folbigg on 14 October 1992 went off without a hitch. Kathy woke Craig early in the morning when her contractions began and he drove her to the John Hunter Hospital in Newcastle. The labour for their third child was relatively quick – less than six hours – and Kathy needed no drugs or forceps to deliver the healthy, blue-eyed, blonde-haired girl. Craig and his sister Carol were both there for the birth. True to form, as with her other children, Kathy stayed in hospital for several days and fed the baby from a bottle before bringing her home to Thornton.

Craig and Kathy had borrowed a wooden sleeping rocker from Carol and an apnoea blanket from the SIDS organisation. The blanket sounded an alarm if it did not detect any motion from the baby after a set period. It quickly became a source of stress for Craig and Kathy because the alarm would beep if Sarah simply held her breath or rolled over or stretched. At night the alarm went off regularly. Kathy would always get up to go and check on her. Neither Kathy nor Craig were entirely sure about how to use the machine and felt they had not been properly instructed on its use, other than following the directions written on the box the blanket had come in.

Craig continued to sleep heavily, as he always had. He even started to sleep through the alarms. In the mornings if he thought Kathy looked 'stuffed or tired' he would ask about the alarm. Her usual reply was: 'The bloody thing went off all night.'

Very quickly after Sarah was born it became clear that Kathy was not coping well with being a full-time mother at home and needed some time to herself. When the baby was two-and-a-half months old Kathy informed Craig that she was 'sick of being broke, sick of being stuck at home' and had got a job working weekends at BabyCo again. Craig could tell that there were parts of motherhood that Kathy enjoyed and others that she did not and recognised that she needed the weekend as her escape after looking after Sarah by herself during the week.

As time progressed and Sarah grew older, Kathy's exasperation with the sleep-apnoea machine increased. Its constant beeping in the night – always with false alarms – was robbing her of sleep. She hated it.

'Bloody thing. Throw it out the window. Do we have to use it?' she asked.

'Of course we do,' said Craig.

Kathy later recalled her experience with Sarah's mat: 'The apnoea mat she was on was a movement mat, not an actual breathing sort of thing. So it would go off if she actually was asleep, not, you know, if she was having a problem of any kind. If she was actually asleep, calm and not moving then the mat would go off and I would have to go in and turn the alarm off and reset it, sort of thing. So it was probably more of a pain than it was worth but we persisted with it . . .'

By contrast Craig found the alarms irritating but comforting.

Never once did Kathy express any concern for Sarah's health or safety in relation to the alarm going off. Craig got the impression that she thought the beeps were always false alarms. Every other day they argued about Kathy's reluctance to continue using the mat.

Kathy nicknamed Sarah the 'catnapper' because she would not sleep for any longer than 15 or 20 minutes at a time. Kathy observed that even during the night she would be lucky to get three hours straight of sleep out of the little girl. Sarah's restless sleeping patterns did not improve as the months went by. The only time she slept happily was when she was in bed with her parents. Later, when asked about Sarah's sleeping patterns, Kathy said: 'Yeah, she would sleep for hours and hours on end if she was in the bed with us but not if she was in a bed by herself. So nine times out of 10 she slept with Craig and I slept in the spare room.' She laughed at that. In years to come Kathy would attribute her own sleep disturbances to her problems with Sarah in 1993.

The constant false alarms and lack of sleep were not the only things annoying Kathy. Craig was now commuting to the Teasdales four-wheel-drive dealership an hour away in Singleton. He was away from home by seven in the morning and found it difficult to get home at a set time, certainly before eight in the evening. He and Kathy fought because he would get home and play boisterously with Sarah – 'revving her up'. Kathy then found it difficult to get her to sleep. Later, when describing this situation, she said of Sarah: 'She was a very loud player. There was lots of screaming and laughing and they would always be trying to chase each other around . . . at that age she was taking delight at running at you and bodily throwing herself at you and you pretty much had to catch her or she'd land on the floor, and that sort of thing . . . play was quite a big thing with her. She, yeah, she always liked to play.'

Kathy further explained her frustration: 'It used to annoy me a little. We used to think she should be sleeping or I'd think to myself she's probably gunna be one grouchy little bugger the next day if she doesn't get some sleep sooner or later. I sort of figured it out real fast that more often than not she would fall asleep with [Craig]. Somewhere along the line she would go to sleep with him so I tended not to let it worry me too much. Unless they were getting very loud and boisterous and just making too much noise that I couldn't get to sleep . . .'

Craig later spoke about the way Kathy acted about Sarah's bedtimes: 'She was a very rigid, regimented type of person and so times were always a factor. So if you went beyond the boundaries of those times, if you got home late, that was tough for you – the baby was going to bed at eight, 8.30pm and that was it. She just got harder about things . . .

'I didn't feel that 8.30pm was a necessary time for this child to go to sleep, if she was playing or whatever, and Kathy used to go off her guts over it, because Kathy wanted this baby to sleep at these times.

'But I was home and it was one thing that was always a contentious issue with us. I was home. I was quite happy to take on that responsibility: bathing her, giving her her dinner, playing with her, putting her to sleep. It was never an issue to me. And that's why we constantly argued over this 8.30 affair. But Kathy could have gone on her merry way and done whatever she wanted to, because I had Sarah.'

At first, while Kathy worked weekends at BabyCo, Craig looked after Sarah but it eventually turned out that he also had to work on Saturday mornings. Sarah was then left with Craig's family – his sister Carol and her husband Robert, or his nephew David and his fiancée. They had all learnt CPR in case Sarah stopped breathing like her brothers had done. However, Craig and Kathy had not undertaken any such training, despite having needed to use it with their other babies. When that babysitting arrangement became too onerous on Craig's family, he took Sarah to work with him. It was only in the middle of 1993 when Carol Newitt's husband told Kathy that she was missing the best parts of her daughter's life that Kathy gave up her weekend escape from the pressures of motherhood. At home full time again Kathy became very frustrated and domineering with Sarah. Once again, Craig heard her growling angrily from time to time.

On Sunday 29 August 1993, Craig and Kathy decided to take Sarah out for the day. She was 10 months old, eating solids, had just learnt to stand and was interacting with the world around her. The family drove to Nobby's Beach in Newcastle where Sarah, despite a runny nose from a slight cold, played in the sand and marvelled at the seagulls. Then the family stopped off at Craig's brother's house before travelling on to the park at East Maitland. Kathy later recounted the events of the day saying it was the 'very first time we decided to take [Sarah] to a park and swings and see grass and other kids and all that sort of thing. She had a ball; she was sort of crawling around and getting into things and so we were nice and relaxed and had a really, really top day'.

They got home to Thornton. It was a normal evening with the regular dinner and bath ritual for Sarah. Kathy later explained: 'One of the fun things she used to like to do was stand at the side of the bath while I was running it and we used to put the old bubbles in and do all that sort of routine and she'd get all excited . . . so bath time used to be a good fun time. She'd have dinner; play with Craig in the evening for quite a while. And, of course, he used to get into trouble for revvin' her up that much. I used to think that partly the reason why she wouldn't go to sleep happily and easily was he used to rev her up that much that she just decided . . . to keep playing and not go to bed . . . I was doing things a little bit differently than what I did with the other two. I did . . . actually try to get her to go to bed . . . between six and seven or up to eight o'clock. I suppose I would try and get her into bed so that she would have a bit of a sleep. Knowing full well she wouldn't have stayed there but at least it was an attempt.'

It was now bedtime and after a full day Kathy was tired. Her mood went downhill fast, even though Craig had been helping her with Sarah. Only in the last couple of days had they decided on a new bedtime routine for Sarah that involved her sleeping in her own single bed at the foot of their bed. Craig had finally relented to Kathy's pleas and abandoned the apnoea mat – three months later than the SIDS organisation had suggested – because they did not think Sarah's movement would pass through the innerspring mattress of the new single bed to the mat beneath. Kathy became frustrated at the prospect that Sarah wasn't going to sleep well that night. This particular night Craig continued to 'rev up' his daughter by videotaping her as she crawled down the hallway towards him and also as she stood in the lounge room playing on her toy organ.

Of that particular Sunday night Craig later said: 'Sarah was all wound up from the day, I suppose, and I had a tendency to wind her up. Kathy took her to put her to sleep and that's when it all went pretty ordinary after that.'

From the lounge room where he was watching TV, Craig could hear Kathy in the bedroom with Sarah, who was crying and grumbling. He could hear his wife patting their daughter to try to comfort her. Suddenly he heard a more disturbing noise. Kathy was growling. He went up to the bedroom and found Kathy on the bed with Sarah pinned to her in a bear hug, a one-armed bear hug. With her other arm she was patting Sarah on the bottom. However, Craig could see it was not a gentle pat. From the doorway he told his wife to mellow out.

'Fuck off!' snapped Kathy, making it clear that she considered she had everything under control.

'Well for Christ's sake, it's World War III between the two of yous every time this kid's got to go to the bedroom. If she doesn't want to go to sleep, why make her go to sleep?' Craig protested.

'Get out!' ordered Kathy. Sarah would go to sleep when she wanted her to.

Craig retreated to the lounge room. He could still hear Sarah was upset and then heard footsteps coming down the hallway. Kathy came through the archway into the lounge room, stopping just short of her husband. Throwing Sarah at him, she barked: 'You fucking deal with her!'

Craig caught his daughter and Kathy stormed off to the bedroom. He cuddled and nursed Sarah on the lounge to stop her crying. Playing with the paper her father had next to him on the lounge, she snuggled into him and eventually fell asleep, breathing heavily and making 'little tiny bubby snores', as Craig called them, in her sleep.

Eventually at around 11 o'clock that night Craig put Sarah into her new single bed in their room, tucking in a sheet and blanket over the sleeping child before getting into bed beside his wife, turning off the light and going to sleep himself. Because she was a boisterous sleeper and would toss and turn and kick in her sleep, Craig and Kathy had placed pillows around her bed in case she fell out.

The next thing Craig remembered was waking up in the middle of the night. He looked at the digital numbers glowing red on the electric clock beside the bed and saw it was 1.10am. Half asleep, he looked around the room. It was obvious that Kathy was not in bed with him. Craig also looked down towards Sarah's bed. His daughter was not in bed either. He looked to the doorway of the bedroom. The door was closed but he could see that a light was shining on the other side of it. He assumed that the light must have been coming from the hallway or vanity and figured that Kathy was looking after Sarah. He could see clearly because the room was flooded with light from the street lamp directly outside the bedroom window. Reassured that Kathy was dealing with Sarah – a perfectly normal nighttime occurrence – Craig went back to sleep.

The next thing Craig knew he was being dragged from his sleep, heart pounding, by Kathy's bloodcurdling scream. The light was now on in the bedroom and he sat bolt upright in bed. Kathy was standing with one hand on the door, screaming. Craig jumped up out of bed and saw Sarah lying in bed on her back, her little legs straight out and her arms alongside her. He had never seen her sleep like that – ever. Normally she would sleep 'crunched up' or with her arms and legs thrown around. Now she looked like a tin soldier on parade. There were no bedclothes covering her. Racing over to his daughter, he picked her up. She felt floppy in his arms. Swinging Sarah around to place her on his bed, he saw the clock. It was 1.34am. Kathy sat in the hallway just outside the door, screaming and crying uncontrollably, with her knees up under her chin.

A little over 20 minutes earlier his wife had been up with Sarah and he had assumed everything was all right. What could possibly have happened in those 20 minutes? Before he had even begun to formulate this question, Craig was trying to save his third child's life.

Sarah was still warm. Craig put his ear to her mouth and listened as hard as he could. She was not breathing. Screaming at Kathy to call an ambulance, he tried to do CPR, blowing into her mouth and nose, and pressing down on her chest. Despite the previous two deaths of his children, Craig's knowledge of CPR was still restricted to what he had read.

Kathy would later give her version of what happened. 'I got up to go to the toilet . . . Because she was in the room with us I sort of just glanced over and saw the little lump in the bed . . . I got up and went to the toilet. When I've walked back in I've took another look at her; she hadn't moved. Probably the only thing that caught my attention was that she was flat on her back and one of her arms just seemed to be hanging out, sort of thing. So I sort of went over just to make sure she wasn't cold or anything, I suppose, and cover her back up again because she kicks all the covers off while she's asleep – she was a bit of a restless sleeper. That's when I noticed again that I wasn't hearing any breath sounds . . . I just sort of woke Craig up and he flicked on a light, I think, that was on the side of the bed, I can't remember now, but there . . . just seemed to be light in the room . . . I cannot remember if I had her or if Craig had her. I remember going into the lounge room. I only remember ringing the ambulance for that one. I remember Craig doing CPR. And then all I remember is the ambulance arriving.'

Kathy was waiting outside for the ambulance while Craig kept breathing into his baby daughter's mouth and nose. According to the logbook at Beresfield Ambulance Station the emergency call was received at the Newcastle Control Centre at 1.24am. The station officer that night was Deborah McDermid. It took her just six minutes to get from the ambulance station located on the New England Highway halfway between Maitland and Newcastle to the Folbiggs' house in Thornton. She was met outside the house by a sobbing Kathy, who directed her to the bedroom.

Officer McDermid ran into the room and told Craig to continue with the CPR. 'Oh, for God's sake, don't stop'. She instructed Kathy to help with the resuscitation efforts while she dashed outside to get more equipment and put a 'Code Two' cardiac-arrest call for additional assistance over the radio. Officer McDermid then rushed back in to take over the resuscitation, directing Craig to move Sarah from the bed to the floor. She noticed that Sarah had mucus and vomit in her mouth, which appeared to be cyanosed, or blue, and that she was not breathing. As the young ambulance officer worked, Craig told her that they had only just stopped using Sarah's apnoea mat.

Another ambulance crew arrived and they joined in the resuscitation, sending Kathy and Craig to wait in the lounge room. The ambulance officers took off

Sarah's little ski suit to administer cardiac drugs directly into the bone at the top of her leg to try to revive her. However, Sarah did not respond to the drugs or therapy they applied.

Forty minutes after she had arrived at the Folbigg home, Officer McDermid came out and told Craig and Kathy the tragic news. Their little girl was dead.

Sarah's little body was brought out to the lounge where Craig nursed her on his lap. The parents were devastated. Sobbing. It had happened again.

Craig telephoned some of his brothers and sisters. Two of them arrived just ahead of two detectives from Maitland Police Station and a police photographer from the Maitland Physical Evidence Section. Ambulance officer Deborah McDermid briefed Detective Stephen Saunders. He could see the parents were very upset, Kathy in particular. Even though he was a detective of 16 years standing he found it very distressing to see her in that state. He was briefed on the family history by Craig's brother before separating Kathy and Craig and questioning them individually in different rooms about the events of the night. Kathy was too upset to give much information. Kathy later spoke about being interviewed that night by the police. 'They sort of came in full force . . . we were a little intimidated by it . . . but we tried to help and answer what we could . . . and that's all I pretty much remember.'

The information Detective Saunders gleaned about what happened that night came from Craig and his brother. Tellingly, the policeman did not regard the investigation as being very thorough. Crucially, his notes differed on the time that Kathy went to the toilet and found Sarah. In his original report it said 1am while in his report to the coroner it said 1.30am.

Craig formally identified Sarah to one of the police officers and they left shortly after. Just before 4am her body was taken to the casualty department of Maitland Hospital by the original ambulance that had attended the emergency. Later that morning ambulance officer McDermid drove back to the house. She had phoned Craig and Kathy to let them know she wanted to prevent them from getting an account for the transport of Sarah from their house to the hospital. The only way she could actually effect that was to turn up at the Folbiggs' house with a form for them to sign. When she got there she saw that Kathy and Craig were both still distressed. They later sent her a thank-you note for being so considerate.

A post-mortem was carried out on Sarah's body by the head of the Institute of Forensic Medicine at Glebe, Professor John Hilton, on the day after she died – 31 August 1993. At the time he did not consider the death to be suspicious. Her body was well nourished and showed no signs of abuse. Professor Hilton noticed that she had two tiny puncture marks on her face below her lower lip and a scratch on her arm. He also noticed that Sarah's uvula, the dangly bit that hangs down the back of the throat, was displaced but he felt Sarah's uvula could have been dislodged as he removed her throat to examine it as part of the post-mortem procedure. Other tests showed no obvious cause of death.

He knew that two of Sarah's siblings had died and that one of them, Caleb, had been diagnosed as having died from SIDS. As with the unexpected death of any infant, Sarah's death was a great cause for concern, and even more so because of the history in her family of a previous death attributed to SIDS.

Professor Hilton rang Craig and Kathy and asked them to come down to meet him at his office in Glebe in Sydney. Craig's sister Carol and her husband, Robert, accompanied them.

They sat in the office and Professor Hilton told them he simply could not understand why their daughter was not running around the office, laughing and giggling with them today. He could find no reason for it. Craig pressed him for more information. There had to be a reason. No, Professor Hilton told him, it was just a terrible case of bad luck. There was no reason that he could see why they should not try to be parents again. He urged them not to let the last three tragedies stand in their way. He gave the cause of death as SIDS because there was no obvious reason why the little girl had died. His decision to attribute Sarah's death to SIDS spared the family from the questions they would have been asked at the inquest they would have had to go through if he had recorded the cause of death as being from unknown or undetermined causes.

Kathy Folbigg was in the clear.

The only questions remaining as to what really happened that morning came from the grieving and deeply distraught Craig. A couple of days after Sarah died he tried to broach some of his concerns with Kathy – that when he had first woken up on the night of Sarah's death, about 20 minutes before Kathy had raised the alarm, he had seen that neither she nor Sarah were in the bedroom. He wanted to know what had happened – why this was so.

'Oh, I got up and went to the toilet. I came back, turned the light on, found her. That was that. The rest you know,' Kathy replied.

That was the end of it as far as Kathy was concerned. She refused to talk to Craig about their children after that. She never mentioned their names again.

Craig's grief overcame everything, all the questions he still wanted to ask Kathy. The nagging doubt was swamped by tears. It was only years later that he would again wonder why his wife had risen from bed to go to the toilet at 1.30am, just over 20 minutes after he knew she had already been out of the room with Sarah.

5

Laura

THE SIX-PAGE HANDWRITTEN letter pulled no punches. It was 1995, two years since the Folbiggs' daughter Sarah had died, and Craig was still grieving. In his shaking hand he held a letter from Kathy, which delivered him an ultimatum. She wanted him to see a grief counsellor or she would leave him. Kathy considered that a separation would be the best thing for Craig. Since Sarah's death he had been a lot more distant and hard to reach. He seemed to be in a world of his own, and Kathy was having a lot of trouble trying to get him to talk to her, let alone anything else.

They had moved several times over the past two years. They had leased their home in Thornton to Craig's nephew and moved up to Singleton. Then Kathy resumed her weekend job at BabyCo in Newcastle so they moved back into the spare room of the house in Thornton so she could reach work more easily. They then bought a new house in Glendale where Craig spent most of his time in the garage rebuilding a red Mini. They had clearly not been able to settle after Sarah's death and had parted then reconciled a few times before Kathy's most recent written ultimatum. Craig's grief manifested itself in the same way that it had after the deaths of his sons, except this time he immersed himself in his work to cope. But still he could not shake the despair so Kathy left him.

Kathy's foster mother, Deirdre Marlborough, was delighted. Kathy knew that her mother and Craig had not seen eye to eye since the time of their wedding. Of her mother's relationship with Craig, Kathy later said: 'She's had a problem with Craig since the first day she met him . . . He will speak his mind if he thinks he has to . . . The thing that really sort of blew it up for them was organising our wedding. She was so thrilled and pleased when I was getting married – that was fine – she liked him up until then. When it came to actually organising the wedding and Craig wanted to use his brother who was in the catering business to make it cheaper for us . . . it became a power struggle then between her and Craig as to who was gunna do what, and they sort of snapped one day and had an argument both in front of me and Dad, and she's never sort of liked him since then. But she was always quick to judge and put him down with his changing of his jobs and all that sort of thing.

'When she thought that we had actually split, she helped get the flat and all the rest of it. I started off with the thought "yes we will split" and I sort of did make a concerted effort to get back into my job and try and get a life of some sort started.'

Craig was back in Singleton by this stage and kept tabs on Kathy from afar as she began to put her life back together in Newcastle. He knew that she had a little flat at Lambton and had formed a fairly strong friendship with his eldest sister, Sherry. Of that time Kathy later said she was enjoying the 'lighter side of life' with Sherry. 'It was a fun sort of relationship. She's a bit of a card; she likes to have a joke. And we were both going to Jenny Craig, the weight-loss centre, because during that course of time I'd actually packed on quite a bit of weight, I was up around the 85kg mark, and she was going to Jenny Craig – she was a life member. So we sort of ended up going there together, then we both ended up going to a gym at Wallsend together. And we sort of hung out a fair bit together . . . she didn't seem to be bothered too much by things.'

Craig could see that Kathy was getting on with her life without him, exercising at the gym and going out dancing at nightclubs with his sister. He missed Kathy desperately and wanted her back so he agreed to see a grief counsellor. Her move away from Craig had worked. Kathy said later: 'That's when he seemed to snap out of it slightly and he must have thought, "my God she's actually gone". And he then started to ring up and I suppose start the courting process if you like, coming to see me, and driving the hour and a half would not bother him – he was always whingeing and complaining if he had to drive an hour and a half anywhere for any reason.'

They began seeing a counsellor, Steel Fitchett, and their relationship started to come together again. Craig had rented a flat in Singleton and Kathy visited for the weekend. Alone together they discussed their marriage in enormous detail. By Sunday night they had decided to give their marriage another try. Kathy returned to Newcastle and found someone to take over her flat in Lambton. She then got a job with electrical-appliance supplier Retravision in Singleton and moved into a rented flat in Aida Street, Singleton, with Craig. She decided not to tell her foster mother that the marriage was back on again but the Marlboroughs learnt of the reconciliation anyway. Kathy later spoke of her foster mother's reaction: 'The price I paid for that was . . . my parents pretty much disowned me once they sort of discovered that Craig and I hadn't actually truly broken up and truly separated and she hasn't spoken to me since.'

Her parents subsequently moved to Darwin for the sake of her foster father's health. Kathy was not told of the move and interpreted her foster mother's actions as a means of punishing her.

Kathy had now not only lost her blood family but also her foster family. Just as she had with the deaths of her three children, she blocked it all out of her mind and moved on. She had Craig and life was good. Now that they had reunited, they borrowed heavily from the bank to buy their dream house, a modern brick-veneer home in Millard Close, Singleton.

It was May 1996. At last, everything seemed to be going swimmingly for the Folbiggs – until Kathy dropped her bombshell. She told Craig how wonderful she felt everything in their life was, that they had a great house and both had good jobs and life was fun. The thing she felt would round it all off was if they had another baby.

Craig was shocked. He felt that they had already discussed and resolved that parenthood was no longer going to be a factor in their marriage, hence the reason they had gone into a huge amount of debt to buy their dream house and were relying on both their wages to pay off the house and then save up to take some trips together.

'No,' he said emphatically.

Kathy was not going to let this go. It was a repeat of the arguments they had had a couple of years ago before Kathy had fallen pregnant with Sarah. 'What is the point of being married if we aren't going to be a family?' asked Kathy.

'No,' said Craig.

'It was wonderful to see you as a dad.'

'No'.

'That was the best time of our lives.'

'No'.

'It was wonderful to be parents together.'

'No'.

Further conversations about Kathy's desire for a baby continued along the same lines. Kathy took a casual, loving and friendly approach. She knew which buttons to push. She knew more than anything else that Craig wanted to be a dad, that he loved having 'bubbies' around. Several years later when Kathy recalled this time she said: 'That time I sort of looked at Craig and thought he really deserves to be a father. He's a natural one; there's not many that you can say are natural dads . . . I'm talking more along the lines of emotional bonding and wanting to help develop your child as in reading to them and spending the quality time. He was really quite good at that. So I just thought . . . it would give him peace and make him truly happy if he was a dad. He was still sort of in his depressions every now and then.'

In an attempt to persuade him that having another baby was a good idea, Kathy continued to soothe and cajole him.

'It can't be that easy,' said Craig. 'You know, you can't just have a baby, come home and play happy families, not with what we have been through.' He was terrified another child would die unexpectedly.

'That won't happen again – we are more mature,

more patient people. Older and wiser,' said Kathy.

Craig erupted. 'Wake up to yourself – what the hell has that got to do with it? Nobody has been able to tell us what happened to our babies, other than at one instance SIDS, and nobody can tell us what SIDS is.'

Later he would remember that odd conversation and realise that SIDS had nothing to do with the children's deaths. Kathy's statement about patience was far more significant. At the time though he was caught in a Kathy-inspired whirlpool of emotion, pressuring him to try for a fourth child with her. He tried to avoid the inevitable. 'Find some people who can help us and then we'll talk about it,' he said.

Life returned to normal for a couple of weeks until Kathy asked Craig if he had been in touch with Professor Hilton yet. The professor was one of the people Craig had suggested she contact before he would further discuss her wish to have another child.

'No, I thought you were going to do that,' he said.

Kathy did not need to talk to experts; she knew it was unlikely there would be anything wrong with the baby.

'Well, you're the one who wants to talk to these people. Why haven't you done it?' she replied.

To keep the peace, Craig called Professor Hilton who in turn referred him to Dr Christopher Seton at the sleep-investigation unit at the Children's Hospital at Westmead in Sydney. Dr Seton already knew of the Folbiggs' circumstances and invited them down to Sydney so he could explain to them the sleep studies and monitoring programs that were conducted at the unit. He welcomed Craig and Kathy into the study and told them there was no reason they should not have another baby. Craig was torn. He badly wanted to be a father but he did not want to go through the pain of losing a child again. Talking to the experts in Sydney began to break down his fears. Technology had advanced and the understanding of SIDS and how to prevent it had also progressed. By the time they left the appointment Craig was feeling a lot more confident. He loved Kathy; they could have a family. Dr Seton wished them luck in getting pregnant. Once again, Craig and Kathy set out to have a baby.

In her own mind, Kathy had also started to think of some safeguards she could put in place to try to protect her next baby from the fate that had befallen her other children. In her diary on 18 June 1996 she wrote:

I'm ready this time and I know I'll have help and support this time. When I think I'm going to lose control like last time I'll just hand baby over to someone else. Not feel totally alone. Getting back into my exercise after will help my state of mind and sleeping, wherever possible as well. I have learned my lesson this time.

By November 1996 Kathy had discovered she was pregnant. On 4 December 1996 she confided more of her feelings about her impending motherhood to her diary:

> I'm ready this time, but have already decided if I get any feelings of jealousy or anger too much I will leave Craig and baby rather than answer being as before. Silly, but will be the only way I will cope. I think support and not being afraid to ask for it will be a major plus. Also, I have and will change my attitude and try earnestly not to let anything stress me to the max. I will do things to pamper myself regularly and just deal with things. If I have a clingy baby, then so be it; a catnapper, so be it. That will be when I will ask for help and sleep whenever I can to keep myself in a decent mood. I know now that battling wills and sleep deprivation were the causes last time.

Kathy went into labour with her fourth child just after midnight on 7 August 1997. Craig drove her to Singleton Hospital where, five hours later, she gave birth to a healthy baby girl. Laura Folbigg was a beautiful baby – the kind any loving parent would wish for. As soon as she was delivered, Craig Folbigg held the tiny blue-eyed, blonde-haired little girl in his arms for a long, long time. Perhaps not quite believing that he was a father again and praying that this time the baby would be all right. Once again, as with the other Folbigg children, Laura scored well on the Apgar test.

The maternity-ward staff at Singleton Hospital took a very firm line with Kathy on the benefits of breast-feeding Laura. Once again, Kathy stayed in hospital with her baby for five days and for that first week mother and daughter succeeded where the other babies had failed and managed to breastfeed success-fully. But her heart was never really in it. She started bottle-feeding Laura once they returned home to Millard Close.

When Laura was just over a week old the family drove down to Sydney to stay overnight at the Royal Alexandra Hospital for Children to get the little girl thoroughly tested for any possible illness or abnorm-ality. They were introduced to clinical-nurse consult-ant Margaret Tanner in the David Reed Sleep Unit and finally were given lessons on the correct way to admin-ister CPR, using a doll to practise on. Laura was fitted to an electronic corometrics monitor and Margaret Tanner explained to them exactly how the machine worked to record and measure the breathing and heartbeat of the child and how it would sound an alarm if there was a cessation of breathing or changes in the regularity of the baby's heartbeat. The machine also recorded periodic breathing, times when the monitor was turned on or off and how many hours it was used during the day. Craig and Kathy were shown how to use the monitor and how to respond to the baby in the event of an alarm by touching her gently so as not to arouse her too much – for example, on the eyelashes – to check whether she responded. The machine could show whether it was a heart alarm, a breathing alarm or a false alarm. The detail of every alarm had to be written on a daily diary sheet. The data recorded on the machine's memory had to be downloaded, weekly at first and eventually monthly, to the hospital via an in-built modem that was plugged into the telephone socket for Ms Tanner to interpret.

The battery of tests carried out on Laura in the neonatal intensive care unit all came back with the same response – she was healthy. She was diagnosed with central apnoea, which was considered to be of no medical significance, unlike obstructive apnoea. It was a breathing disorder that she would grow out of and it offered no risk to her. She was effectively a very healthy, normal child. What perhaps was not so normal was the way her mother behaved. Ms Tanner observed that Kathy did not act in the same way as other parents who had lost a baby to SIDS. Ms Tanner expected Kathy, if anything, to be overprotective. The relationship between mother and daughter appeared difficult; to Margaret Tanner Kathy seemed detached, as if she did not want to get close to Laura. The clinical-nurse consultant later said of Kathy: 'She wasn't watching [Laura]. She would go out and have a cigarette or go out and have a break quite often.'

In contrast, she said of Craig: 'Craig was terrified.

He also went out and had a lot of cigarettes. He was terrified, frightened, totally the opposite.' He needed to be reassured that his daughter was healthy and that they had the very best technology to keep her alive.

Kathy later said: 'We were very optimistic by the time we left the hospital that we had one that breathed and slept properly and there was no sort of dramas and she was . . . more of a sedate, relaxed baby. There didn't seem to be much that would worry her.' Reassured by their visit to the hospital and the consultation with Margaret Tanner, Craig was more involved with Laura when they returned home to Singleton than he had been with any of the other children. Kathy remembered this time later: 'He had lots more to do with her in general than the other three. He was always holding her and would quite often feed her . . . the changing of her was a bit of a problem; we used to have to get him forcibly to do that.' Craig felt much more hopeful now that he knew they had a healthy daughter and was keen to be involved – at least during the day. Kathy was still left with sole responsibility at night.

Laura slept in a bassinette next to her parents' bed. The electrodes of the monitor were strapped to her body and the wire left dangling so that she could be plugged into the machine whenever she had a nap. 'There was no question about that; it was on every time she slept, even if it was only for a 15-minute nap or whatever, she would have it on,' said Kathy, when speaking a couple of years later about using the alarm. 'The alarm was quite sensitive. It was actually programmed for a full second; if she wasn't actually breathing for even less than a full second . . . it would sound off. It was quite ear piercing and would even wake Craig up so I was a bit more relaxed that way that when it went off he actually stirred. It wasn't something that he could sleep through, but I had the monitor and everything directly next to me and next to the bed and she was placed so that if it went off, if I stood up I could see her. I was pretty much on top of her to see what was going on. Craig rarely answered the monitor because he was over the other side of the bed so it was usually me that did it.'

The monitor was certainly protecting little Laura, but not in the way Craig or the experts, nurses and doctors at Westmead intended. In her diary on 25 August 1997, 18 days after Laura was born, Kathy confided:

> Scary feelings. I've realised I actually love her and have bonded with her. Wish to protect her etcetera. Maternal instinct is what they call it. I now know I never had it with the others. Monitor is a good idea. Nothing can happen without the monitor knowing and since I'm not game enough to not plug it in because they'd want to know why I hadn't, everything will be fine this time.

The monitor was keeping Laura alive because it was

keeping Kathy honest. Nurse Margaret Tanner in Sydney was keeping a close eye on all the data that was regularly sent down from Singleton by the Folbiggs.

By the time Laura was six weeks old, life had settled into a routine with Craig getting used to the alarm and sleeping through it while Kathy dealt with the baby alone. On 20 September 1997 Kathy wrote in her diary:

> Sleep. Who needs it? Yes, I'm getting a little bit irritable now. This is my punishment for the others, to be continually woken up, because this time we know that we have a child with a sleeping disorder. Even though I'm sure they are all false alarms, the thought is still scary. Am getting very stressed because I can't depend on Craig for any real support or help. He doesn't hear her or the alarms. How dare he complain to me about lack of sleep? What the fuck would he know? Think he'll have to sleep in the other room, just so he's not disturbed. Selfish prick. Well now I know where I stand. Craig is refusing to help and hasn't even attempted to in any way. Just wants me to bear all the stress so he can keep selling his cars and making money. I suppose the stress of having to provide for us is real, but it's nothing compared to this.

Even though Craig insisted on the monitor being turned on at night, Kathy started to become slack about using it when she and Laura were home alone. She stopped plugging it in during the day. Ms Tanner had already noticed that by the second week after the Folbiggs had taken Laura home the use of the monitor was 'very scant' during the day.

The clinical-nurse consultant later reported: 'The next fortnight was even more scant and the fortnight after that . . . we went a whole month and the only time it was used during the day was on one Sunday and on one Monday in the month.' After that, the only time the monitor was turned on during the day coincided with Craig's holidays or weekends at home. Craig recognised too that Kathy's use of the monitor was sporadic. He later recalled: 'I was doing the downloads and I would come home at the appropriate time that Westmead had told us and hook it all up and dial through for the download and I was reading the day diaries, and I noticed that there was some significant amounts of time which were missing, which were daytime, from the diary.'

Craig was perturbed by this and confronted Kathy. 'Why aren't you plugging Laura in of a day?' he said.

'Well, I keep my eye on her; I put her down for a sleep and I just check on her and she's fine,' Kathy replied.

'Well, that's not what they told us. You're going to go and do something; if this thing happens, it happens pretty quickly.'

'It's driving me mental! I just want to have a normal baby.'

76

'Well, she's not normal. Until they tell us she's normal, she's not normal,' said Craig.

It was almost as if Kathy did not take the risk seriously. Did not think Laura could stop breathing in her sleep just as her brothers and sister had. Every time Craig brought the subject up Kathy would become very angry. He later described that she would 'go off her head, tell me it wasn't me who had to put up with it and all that sort of stuff. I was very worried about it and so I wrote a letter.' This letter was sent to nurse Margaret Tanner at Dr Seton's clinic on 18 March 1998 when Laura was almost seven months old. It read:

Dear Margaret,

I hope this letter finds you well. Kathy, Laura and I are fine. Laura is going great guns now that she has shaken all the little bugs she had. She is in the process of learning to crawl at the moment and does not like it one bit. 'Why crawl when mum or dad can carry me or get things for me?' I bet that's what she thinks. We had Pixie photos done and I hope you don't mind but I have sent you one. I'm sorry it isn't any bigger, but at least it won't get bent in the mail.

Our last report on Laura's sleep studies was very good and I was pleased to see that Chris [Seton] wanted the home monitoring to continue.

I personally find the flashing lights of the machine comforting, although the alarms are frightening as you are totally unaware of what awaits you when you get to Laura. Happily so far all has been fine. Strangely though I feel that Kathy finds it all tedious and frustrating and would probably rather not use it at all, merely entrusting Laura's survival to fate. You would think that after all she had been through as a mother she of all people would be more diligent with the monitoring.

Is it necessary that Laura be monitored through her daytime sleeping as I'm more than sure that Kathy does not do this. Have you noticed this on the downloads?

I'm sorry if I sound paranoid, but with every passing day I fall that much further in love with this child and truly could not bear her not being a part of my life.

We will be seeing Chris Seton in May some time and I am preparing a list of questions to bring up in our discussion with him then.

Anyway, I didn't mean for this letter to be anything more than a hello and a thank you once again, for all your help so far. I look forward to talking to you on our next download.

Sincerely yours
Craig, Kathy and Laura.

Craig need not have worried so much at this stage. Kathy loved Laura because of her lovely nature and knew that the monitor had little to do with keeping her daughter alive. She wrote in her diary on 25 October 1997:

Just watched video of Sarah. Little upsetting but she did some funny things. Made us laugh. Think John [Craig's brother] was a little upset but he hid it well. I looked at it but have to be honest and say I cherish Laura more. I miss her, yes, but I'm not sad that Laura is here and she isn't. Is that a bad way to think? Don't know. I think I am more patient with Laura. I take the time to figure what is wrong now, instead of just snapping my cog. Also, she is a far more agreeable child and is easy most of the time. Not sure how Craig feels about Sarah now. Know that even though he tried, he loves Sarah just as hard and wasn't prepared for that. I thought he could remain standoffish, but couldn't. I think Laura is beautiful compared to Sarah. She was cute, but Laura has a special look about her. Her slight difference in looks gives her a beautiful face, not just pretty, cute and cuddly, gorgeous and beautiful. Well, so far anyway. Looking at the video, Sarah was boyish looking. Laura has definitely feminine features. They are chalk and cheese, and, truthfully, just as well. Wouldn't have handled another one like Sarah. She saved her life by being different.

The arguments between husband and wife continued over Kathy's inconsistent use of the monitor. She eventually felt that she had worn down Craig into 'reluctant agreement' to reduce the use of the monitor during the day. However, they continued to use it through the night.

Craig spoke later about the stress the monitor's alarms caused. 'There was one night we had a huge amount [of false alarms]. It transpired at the end of the day, of the night. In the early hours of the morning we discovered why. It was because . . . the breathing button that stuck to Laura was too low on her body, but that was a terrible night,' said Craig.

Craig also said later that he had tried to help Kathy when the alarm went off in the night. 'Over and over and over again during this time of corometrics monitoring of Laura I would attempt to get out of bed and Kathy would say to me: "It's okay, I'll deal with it."'

He had insisted: 'No, it's okay, I'll have a go.'

'No, it's fine, I'll do it,' Kathy had repeated.

The only one of the Folbiggs who was sleeping soundly was Laura. When the alarms went off, she might have been disturbed slightly but she would always go straight back to sleep. Later Kathy said: 'She was a really good, good baby. There was no sort of trouble with her at all.'

However, in her diary Kathy had acknowledged that things were going wrong. On 16 January 1998, when Laura was only five months old, she wrote of how she longed for a life away from her husband and daughter:

> Been daydreaming again about life on my own. Wild, highly exaggerated as if I could or really want to. Always seem to when not really happy. Sorry to say I don't get excited any more. Craig just doesn't do it for me any more. Has to be because of this last pregnancy, plus I'm tired all the time. Want to do nothing but sleep. It's not Craig; it's me. Plus we don't get to go out to dinner or dancing together any more. There isn't much — well, there's no romance between us any more. It's all let's make money and raise Laura. We've forgotten ourselves in the process. Sad how that happens. One of my problems is I've lost me again. I'm just Mrs Craig Folbigg. No I'm just Laura's mother as well. Where's Kath gone, a person in her own right who needs to have writing lessons, but probably better if I don't. Then no one, not even me, will be able to read this when I'm gone.

At that stage Kathy took out her frustration on her daughter. On 20 January 1998 she wrote:

> Very depressed with myself, angry and upset. I've done it. I've lost it with her. I yelled at her so angry that it scared her. She hasn't stopped crying. Got so bad I nearly purposely dropped her on the floor and left her. I was restrained enough to walk away. Went to my room and left

81

her to cry. Was gone probably only five minutes, but it seemed like a lifetime. I feel like the worst mother in this earth. Scared that she'll leave me now like Sarah did. I knew I was short tempered and cruel sometimes to her and she left with a bit of help. I don't want that to ever happen again. I actually seem to have a bond with Laura. It can't happen again. I'm ashamed of myself. I can't tell Craig about it because he'll worry about leaving her with me. Only seems to happen if I'm too tired. Her moaning, bored, whingey sound drives me up the wall. I truly can't wait until she's old enough to tell me what she wants.

The next meeting the Folbiggs had with Dr Seton in May went well and, with the most common danger time frame for SIDS victims now past, he suggested they could return the monitor. Craig, however, wanted to keep it for a few more months.

Laura's first birthday was celebrated in August with a massive party around the Folbiggs' giant backyard pool. Laura had managed to live longer than any of her siblings and that was a cause for celebration.

'When she reached her first birthday it was the biggest party you have ever seen in your life. We sort of, it was just a humungous big party out the back with all these friends, and better than you'd give an adult probably, but we were just so happy that she had reached one,' Kathy later said.

Margaret Tanner came up from Sydney and told

them they could keep the corometrics monitor for a little longer if they liked. Certainly Laura's survival was due to two things: the monitor – which Craig was still keen to use if only for his own peace of mind – and the child's placid nature.

Laura did not even trouble her mother by getting ill. Kathy later said: 'There had been no other problems during that first 12 months other than when she . . . had her first cold; during the first cold season she had come up with the sniffles a couple of times. Nothing ever serious and she always soldiered through it and it didn't last very long. It wasn't something that hung on for days on end . . . Always with her, if she had the sniffles of any kind or even coughed just once Craig, and I would go to the doctors, you know. So whether it was needed or not, we'd decided that . . . we weren't taking any chances.'

The most sick Laura had been was in June 1998 when she had been admitted to Singleton Hospital overnight with mild croup. Although the doctor who examined her felt there was no cause for concern, he admitted her for observation overnight primarily because of her history, and the history of her siblings.

According to the family general practitioner, Dr Paul Innes, Laura was a normal, healthy child with no chronic illnesses. She was treated for the usual viral complaints, a rash that was attributed to hives and for a slight fever. The practice nurse also gave Laura her immunisations. The only treatment Laura received that was out of the ordinary was for a second-degree burn after she grabbed the spit roast at a family barbeque. Doctors could see no hint of abuse. Dr Innes later said: 'We are taught to be on the lookout and there was nothing that I can recall that would have alarmed me about her presentation. In fact, when you look at the two, four, six, eight visits relating to the burn, that shows that there was a concern to make sure that the child was getting the right treatment for that particular condition.'

Laura was thriving. In December 1998, when she was 16 months old, the Children's Hospital asked the Folbiggs to return the corometrics monitor. Any danger of SIDS had passed and there were other newborn babies who needed the monitor more. Reluctantly, Craig drove down to Sydney to take it back. Kathy later said: 'For the first, probably, month . . . I didn't sleep too well while she was off the monitor and Craig actually slept lightly, which is the first time he's ever done that in years. Only because we would listen so intently . . . We'd hear everything, even what the neighbours were doing outside.' But while Laura's health and growth was going from strength to strength, the relationship between her parents had been going rapidly downhill ever since Laura had started walking at around 11 months and becoming more independent. Kathy was becoming more and more irritable with Craig and angry with Laura when she did not do as she was told.

Craig later spoke of the growing tension: 'It was getting worse. Our relationship had fairly much packed it in. We were pretty much both living for Laura, or so I thought. Most of the time we slept in separate rooms . . . I used to say to people that I lived with my daughter's mother. That was the basis of our relationship. It was cordial; it was polite if you keep your mouth shut, didn't aggravate or intimidate her. You pretty much got left alone.'

If Craig kept to himself his opinion about Kathy's daily trips to the gym and weekly nights out with the girls there would be no scenes.

By the time Laura was 18 months old things were much worse. Kathy was filling in as a holiday-relief worker at Retravision and was frustrated that the Kathy who loved to go to the gym and party at night-clubs was secondary to Kathy the wife and mother. She decided to tackle her relationship with Craig head on and, as she felt she communicated better through letters and diaries than verbally, wrote her husband a letter saying that she wanted to call it a day and end the marriage. She told him that she could not communicate with him. In one part she wrote: '*Over the years you have become an oppressive and depressing person. I only see sparks and tiny ones at that of the man that attracted me all those years ago.*'

The letter hit hard. Craig considered the letter and went to speak to her about it, admitting that he had been cranky and uncommunicative.

'Finally you talk to me,' said Kathy.

Craig told her that he thought the marriage could be saved, that there were ways to reinvigorate it to keep them together. He was horrified when Kathy told him that although she wanted to go off by herself she planned to take Laura and leave her somewhere she thought her daughter would be safe until she returned. She was not planning to leave Laura with him.

'You can pack your bags and go at any time you like, but you are not taking that child out of this house. This is Laura's home and I am her dad. Every time you leave me, you devastate me. If you leave me again not only will I be devastated by losing you, but also that you've taken Laura,' said Craig.

'I will not walk out of this house and leave that child,' his wife replied.

'Well you have a problem,' Craig barked back.

'I will not ever have anybody tell me I'm no better than my mother.'

'Well, we better sit down and work this out,' said Craig.

They sat down that night and talked for hours, venting their feelings and agreeing to be more considerate of each other's needs. Kathy expressed that part

86

of her frustration was caused by the fact that she never felt she had enough time to herself. She was upset that Craig made her feel bad for leaving Laura with friends so she could do something for herself and go to the gym. She asked if Craig could make more of an effort to get home on time so as to watch Laura while she went out and had some time to herself. Craig agreed that he would do his best to make this happen. Happy that they had managed to reach a resolution, the couple finally ended the discussion with an embrace.

Craig Folbigg loved his wife. Deeply. He was besotted by her. A few days later, on 17 February 1999, he sat down and typed her a reply to her letter. In part he wrote:

Through good times and bad, through richer or poorer, through sickness and in health, as long as we both shall live, these words I hold true as they were my oath to you. I love you and desire you with every fibre of my being and I am proud of your achievements, with your weight loss and your efforts in those regards. I am immensely proud of the mother you are to Laura. It is something I have wished for a long time.

They were the words he felt Kathy would have liked to hear. After he finished typing Craig sat back and re-read the letter. He felt unsettled. Something, he felt, did not ring true. A small seed of doubt at the back of his mind niggled at him. He could not bring himself to give the letter to his wife. His doubt was about to be justified – in the cruellest possible way.

6

Unlucky Last

CRAIG PULLED INTO the driveway. It was late on a Friday afternoon, about two weeks after he had moved back from the spare room to his wife Kathleen's bedroom. He was relieved that he and Kathy were trying to patch up their marriage because he did not want 19-month-old Laura growing up in a home where her mum and dad slept apart. It had hurt him to hear her wandering down the hallway, pointing out the different bedrooms as 'Daddy's room and Mummy's room'. All that mattered to Craig was that 'bubby' was safe and well and happy. She had given him back everything he had thought he lost when his other three children had died. Nothing else mattered. He valued every moment with Laura because his time with her brothers and sisters had been so short.

Walking into the house to greet his wife and daughter he found Kathy getting ready to go out. He knew it was pointless to try to get her to spend the evening at home with him; to keep her from wanting to leave him he knew he had to let her have some time to herself. So while Kathy went out for a night on the town with the girls to blow off steam he stayed home and looked after Laura.

Predictably, Kathy was still asleep after getting home late when Craig woke up at six the following morning to get Laura up, give her breakfast and muck about with her. At quarter to eight, after getting ready for work at the Land Rover dealership in town, he went into the bedroom to ask Kathy to get up to look after Laura so he could leave.

'Just let her run around the house; she'll be all right,' Kathy replied from bed.

'You can't do that, just let a baby run around the house alone!' said Craig. Kathy relented and got out of bed.

Craig returned home from work at midday. His hand-restored classic Mini was entered into a car show downtown and he wanted to take his family to see it. Kathy had other ideas though. She had hired a stack of videos and didn't want to devote the afternoon to her husband's hobby. Nor would she let him take Laura because there would be too many people at the show. She knew Laura would get over-excited and then become irritable. Kathy did not want to have to deal with that; it was not worth the time she would get to herself while Craig and Laura were out. 'She'll get all grumpy. You'll bring her home and I'll have to deal with her.'

It was the same story when Craig returned at 2.30pm. It was a sunny Saturday afternoon and he wanted to take the family on a drive. Again, Kathy didn't want to go out and she also refused to let him take Laura. 'No, you can't take her. She'll be too tired when you get her home. Just go on your own,' Kathy told him. So he did. And he enjoyed it rather more than he expected, rushing back home to spend the last 40 minutes with Laura before her 8.30pm bedtime. But when he got in Laura was already in bed.

Odd.

Out of habit Craig got up at six again on Sunday morning. Half an hour later he heard the usual 'Dad, Dad, Dad' down the hallway. He fetched Laura, made her toast, gave her a bottle and played with her around the house. Sometime before nine Kathy emerged. There was a strange tension in the air. Craig noticed almost immediately that Laura and Kathy were having nothing to do with each other. It seemed that they were avoiding contact.

Something was wrong.

Kathy complained that she was sick of being stuck in the house and told Craig she wanted to go out for a drive. Pointing out that he had been for a drive the day before, he suggested they organise a barbeque with her friends instead. Kathy seemed pleased with this idea and got on the phone and arranged for their friends Dean and Tanya Schmidt to come over with their three children. The Folbiggs hopped in the car, paid a visit to some other friends who had just started their own business, and went to Woolworths to buy the food for the barbeque.

Once the Schmidts arrived Craig and Dean took charge of supervising the children. Craig took a video of Laura playing with Dean and Tanya's son Nicholas in the pool in the back garden while Tanya stayed outside the fenced-off area with their other son, Nathan, and new baby, Sarah. Kathy spent much of the day inside preparing meals for everyone. Laura was full of beans that sunny Sunday afternoon. She ran, screamed, laughed and swam with her bright orange floaties on her arms. As Craig took the video she impishly returned to investigate the pool-filter cover while he indulgently told her to stop, time and time again. Her smile and golden hair lit up the afternoon.

After the Schmidts left, Craig bathed Laura and then together with Kathy gave her some dinner before bed. The three of them watched television together and played hide-and-seek before Kathy put Laura to bed. It had been a wonderful day – only Craig was still feeling troubled. Something was not right and he brought it up with his wife. 'What's going on between you and Laura? You know, you haven't been near her all day. The kid's kept away from you. Every time you have gone to go near her she's just come running to me.'

'Oh, she's got the shits with me,' said Kathy.

'How does a baby have the shits with its mother?'

'It's probably what I did to her last night.'

'Well, what did you do to her?'

'I lost it with her.'

'What do you mean you lost it with her?'

Kathy told him that while he was away on Saturday Laura had been following her around the house, whingeing, moaning, and repeatedly saying, 'Mum, Mum, Mum'. Kathy had lost her cool. 'Piss off,' she had shouted, spinning around quickly. Not realising how close the child was, Kathy had knocked her over.

Nineteen-month-old Laura had lain on the ground in terror, an emotional wreck. Kathy told Craig that the sight of this upset her and she had sat down with the child to calm her down. 'I settled her down and put her to bed. Then you came home, and I went to bed as well,' she finished.

Craig was stunned. He could not believe what he was hearing. 'Good on you,' were the only words he could find to say to his wife.

At 6 o'clock on Monday morning Craig awoke to start a new working week. Laura woke up 20 minutes later and they got up together. Craig made his daughter toast while watching the morning news on television. Kathy emerged at quarter to seven and

Craig noticed Laura becoming very clingy with him as he went about his normal routine of getting ready for work. Picking up the subdued and whingy toddler, he walked around the house, nursing her in his arms. They fed the goldfish and the lid of the tank fell off, hitting Laura on the shoulder, bringing on more tears. Angrily Kathy told Craig to put the child down. Laura followed her father into his bedroom and started jumping on the bed. Craig took her off and she ran away down the hallway crying. As he continued to potter around before work he could hear Kathy losing patience with their daughter. Then it came. A growl, a deep guttural roar. Craig had heard it increasingly, almost daily over recent months when Kathy became frustrated with Laura over bedtimes and mealtimes, and as she became angry with Craig about his attitude as they fought. It was a terrifying, angry sound. Petrifying to a small child and alarming enough to bring Craig straight out from the bedroom.

Kathy had placed Laura in her highchair in the dining room. She had pinned the toddler's hands to the surface of the highchair with her own hand and was trying to feed Laura cereal with her other hand. Forcefeeding. Laura's head was twisting and turning as she whined in protest.

'For Christ's sake, she's a bloody baby. If she doesn't want to have breakfast, don't bother trying to make her,' cried Craig.

'Fuck off!' shouted Kathy. Laura would have her breakfast when she was told.

'You're fucking unreal, Kathy. I just can't figure this out.'

'She's only like this when you're around. You do this to her. You mollycoddle her and sook her up too much.'

'It's better than having her cry.'

Kathy was not going to tolerate this. She grabbed Laura and dragged her from the highchair, plonking her on the ground. 'Go to your fucking father,' she yelled.

As Laura darted across the room Kathy's frustration boiled over into a growl that transformed into a roar of rage. She threw her arms into the air and screamed: 'I can't handle her when she's like this!' The rage filled the room. Laura dropped to the ground in abject terror, unable to move another step to the safety of her father's arms. Stepping forward, Craig scooped up his daughter and tore down the hall to the bedroom. He sat on the bed with her, trying to soothe the toddler. Laura was hysterical, shaking and sobbing on his lap. Gently he hugged her and rocked her, trying desperately to settle her down. 'Mummies and daddies argue. It doesn't mean they don't love you,' he cooed.

Moments later Kathy was at the bedroom door.

'Give me that baby.'

'Just fuck off,' said Craig.

'You give me that baby and you get ready for work. Get out! You do this. This is your fault,' said Kathy. By now she had stormed into the room and had grabbed Laura by one arm. Craig still had hold of her in his lap.

'Kath, just let her go. Just leave her. Piss off,' he said. 'You look like you're going to punch somebody.'

'If I was going to punch anybody I'd punch you. Just give me that bloody baby,' snarled Kathy.

Craig released his hold and followed his wife and daughter back down the hall. 'Bugger off and get ready for work,' Kathy snapped.

He showered and dressed for work, all the time listening intently for what was happening with his wife and daughter. By the time he was ready to leave things had calmed down and Kathy met him at the breakfast bar. She pointed through to the family room. 'Look, she's fine now. She's just watching TV.' Laura was sitting on her small Bananas in Pyjamas lounge with a bowl of dry cereal, watching 'The Teletubbies'. 'She's fine. She's only like this when you're around. Just go to work.'

He complied with his wife's request. It had already been one hell of a day. What Craig Folbigg did not know was that it was about to get a whole lot worse.

Craig was sitting at his desk at Teasdales at 8.30am when his direct line rang. 'Hi sweetheart, it's me,' said

Kathy. She had a playful lilt to her voice; she was chirpy and sounded very loving.

Odd.

'Yes, what do you want?' asked Craig, perplexed.

'I just wanted to ring you to have a talk. I think when you get home we have to have a talk about our life. About us,' said Kathy. She then apologised for losing her temper that morning.

'Well, you know, you can't go on like that. It's not healthy,' replied her husband.

Kathy knew that. She explained that it all came down to their different parenting methods and they needed to talk about it. 'You're too soft on her. You let her get away with too much. You sook her up too much. And that's why she's how she is,' she said. 'Laura is fine now; she's watching TV. We're about to go out to the gym.'

'Well, why don't you come in and have morning tea with me?'

Kathy sounded hesitant. 'I'll see how I go.'

'No. If you say Laura's fine and you're fine, come in and have morning tea with me,' urged Craig, before saying goodbye.

Fitness instructor Kerrie Anderson worked at the BodyFlex gym in Singleton and arrived for work five minutes late at 9.05 that Monday morning. Kathy was waiting for her at the gateway of the childminding area. Her aerobics class had already begun and she immediately left for it as soon as she had deposited Laura. Kerrie and Kathy knew each other quite well and often had coffee after fitness sessions. Kerrie had been told about the other three Folbigg children by Kathy who had asked her to keep a special eye on Laura. Today Kerrie noticed that Laura seemed to be mostly over the cold that had been troubling her over the past week and that the little girl was playing hard with two other children among the 11 that were in the crèche that morning.

At 10.35am Kathy returned from her aerobics session and changed Laura's nappy. She turned down Kerrie's offer of coffee because Laura would 'just run around'; she told Kerrie her daughter was tired and needed a sleep. Kathy left the gym with Laura and headed to Teasdales.

Craig was sitting at his desk in his upstairs office of the car dealership when Kathy dropped Laura in. 'There you go. Go and talk to your dad,' she told the child before going out to make herself and Craig a coffee and chat to one of Craig's female workmates. Laura was delighted to be at work with her daddy. She was giggly and happy, and was very active. Beautiful in flowery bike shorts and a yellow T-shirt, she sat on her dad's lap at his desk and drew him pictures. Pictures that Craig would find when he next came to work and would fold and place in a frame behind a photograph of Laura as a treasured memory of those precious moments that he spent with his beloved daughter.

'I better get buggerlugs home; she's due for a sleep,' Kathy told him after they had been at his office for an hour.

'Okay, no worries,' said Craig. But Laura did not want to go. She clung to her father.

'I'll go without you. I'll go without you,' joked Kathy, pretending to walk away. Craig picked up Laura and carried her to the gate, kissing his wife and daughter goodbye. They crossed the road to the car and Kathy strapped Laura into her child seat. Waving to Craig, they drove off.

That was the last time Craig saw Laura alive.

After Kathy left, Craig went back to his desk and took a call from his nephew Daniel. They had been on the phone catching up for 25 minutes when a young man from the spare-parts department burst into the office and screamed at Craig that he had to hang up.

Something had happened to Laura. He had to get to the hospital. Now.

Craig jumped into his car and roared to the district hospital a couple of kilometres away in Dangar Road. He burst through the doors of the casualty ward and a hospital worker met him. She led him along a corridor and downstairs as he tried to get her to tell him what had happened, what was wrong. The hospital worker told Craig that she could not tell him. Then he heard Kathy crying. When he got into the waiting room he saw her being comforted by a nurse.

'Where's Laura?' he asked.

Kathy pointed to a door opposite. The sight that greeted Craig as he walked in was his and every other parent's worst nightmare. Tiny golden-haired Laura was lying on a hospital bed surrounded by ambulance officers and a doctor who was packing away his equipment.

'You can't stop. What are you doing? You can't stop!' screamed Craig.

'I'm sorry, Mr Folbigg, but she's gone,' said the doctor.

Craig was overwrought. A nurse grabbed him and led him back to the waiting room where Kathy was still sitting.

'I called you. Where were you? Why didn't you come home? I called you,' cried Kathy through her tears.

'I didn't get any phone call,' said Craig, who was now also weeping. 'What happened?'

'I just went in and she was just lying there,' Kathy told him.

As the shock sank further in, Craig asked his wife again what had happened in the time since she had left his office with their happy, healthy daughter.

Kathy told him how on the two-and-a-half-kilometre drive back home Laura had fallen asleep. When she pulled up in the driveway, Laura had remained asleep. Kathy carried the sleeping child through to her bedroom, taking off Laura's favourite Teletubby sandals in the hallway, before laying down the little girl on her bed. She then went outside and played with the dog, cleaned up the veranda and hung out the washing. Because of what had happened to their other three children the Folbiggs had a listening monitor they used to keep a check on Laura. Kathy told her husband that she had heard Laura cough and splutter on the monitor but did not rush in straight away to see what was wrong. First she finished what she was doing and then five or 10 minutes later went in to Laura's bedroom to check on her. The child was pale and her lips were slightly blue and felt cool to the touch. Kathy picked her up and raced into the kitchen. With Laura laid out on the breakfast bench, Kathy said she started to perform CPR while frantically trying to get through to Craig on the telephone and also call an ambulance.

It only took two minutes from the time Kathy placed the 000 emergency call for the ambulance to arrive. Ambulance officer Brian Wadsworth entered the house with colleague Harold Picton to find Kathy administering CPR on Laura. Kathy was crying. The ambulance officers immediately sprang into action, checking Laura for signs of life. The child was not breathing and they could find no pulse. Taking over the CPR, the officers fitted Laura to an intravenous line and monitored her heart with an ECG monitor. They picked up an occasional blip of a heartbeat amid the machine's flatline readout. With a tiny electrical pulse there was still hope. They rushed Laura into the ambulance and sped to the hospital while maintaining their resuscitation attempts.

It was not to be. Shortly after the ambulance officers handed Laura over to the hospital staff, the doctors pronounced her dead.

It had happened again – the Folbiggs had lost another child.

As the news spread, Craig's family came to offer support and rallied around the inconsolable couple. Friend and neighbour Melissa Smith, whose own son, Mark, had died of Sudden Infant Death Syndrome in 1998, rushed to the hospital. She found Kathy sitting in a chair, shaking and crying hysterically. The sight distressed Mrs Smith. It was the only time Kathy's distress would distress an onlooker: she never showed any emotion for Laura again.

Roughly five hours later, at 5pm, the Folbiggs were allowed to go home, after the police had investigated the house as was standard procedure whenever a child had died. Craig was grief-stricken. Devastated. Laura's presence still filled the house. There on the futon were the Teletubby sandals she had been given for Christmas and had been wearing in his office only hours before.

Odd.

On the futon. Not in the hallway outside her bedroom where Kathy had told him she had taken them off and left them. And there in the family room was the monitor plugged into the wall where it usually sat for them to check on their beloved daughter.

Odd.

Kathy had told him she had heard Laura's cough through the monitor while she was out at the clothes-line. But there was the monitor in the family room where it usually sat – a long way from the clothesline.

That night, Monday 1 March 1999, Craig and Kathy began the heartbreaking task of picking up Laura's things and packing them away in her bed-room. Craig, angry and desolate, watched as his wife took down every photograph of Laura on display, and the few photographs of their other children, and packed them away. Out of sight.

Again, odd.

But if Craig Folbigg was beginning to think that a few things were not quite right, he was not alone. Another man he had met that day had been troubled by the events surrounding little Laura Folbigg's death. And Detective Bernie Ryan was not the kind of man to let those things pass without closer examination.

7

Suspicion

IT WAS A ROUTINE MATTER. A child had died and as a matter of course a police officer from Singleton Police Station had been assigned to look into it. On Monday 1 March 1999 Detective Senior Constable Bernie Ryan was on duty in Singleton and given what, at that stage, seemed a standard assignment, albeit a tragic one. He was 31 years old with tenacity, talent and ambition but very little opportunity to exercise those skills on the quietly rural Singleton police beat. He had headed down to the Singleton District Hospital, taken an update from Senior Constable Robinson, who was already there, and then walked into the room where Kathleen and Craig Folbigg were grieving the loss of their daughter Laura.

It was clear to him that the couple was extremely distraught and Detective Ryan wanted to help them as much as he could. He had a brief chat with hospital staff and was told of the family's tragic history – that three other children had already died.

Detective Ryan kept an open mind as he approached

Kathy. His professional training had taught him to weigh all the evidence before reaching any conclusions. He approached her with all the sensitivity his training and basic humanity could muster.

'Can you tell me what happened with Laura today?' he gently inquired.

Through her tears Kathy began her account. 'She woke up at 6.20 this morning. She was in a bad mood. Craig went to work and we had breakfast. We went to the gym and then we went to see Craig at work for morning tea. She went to sleep in the car on the way home, so I put her into bed when we got home. I heard her coughing and did not think much of it. I went to check on her about five minutes later and saw that she wasn't breathing. I took her to the breakfast bar and did CPR and rang 000.'

'Why was Laura in a bad mood?' the detective asked.

'She's had a cold for about a week now,' said Kathy.

'What was Laura wearing this morning?'

'Flower bike shorts and a yellow T-shirt,' said Kathy. She went on to explain to Detective Ryan that she had left the gym at 10.30am and got back from Craig's work at 11am.

'How long after you put Laura to bed did you hear her coughing?' he asked.

'Half an hour.'

'What did you see when you walked into Laura's room to check on her?'

'She was lying on her back and her face was all white.'

Kathy was obviously upset. Detective Ryan, filled with sympathy at this stage and perhaps thinking of his own daughter of a similar age to Laura, moved on to talk to the father.

His chat with Craig Folbigg was brief but emotional. Craig told him that Laura was the fourth child the couple had lost. The conversation and circumstances moved the detective greatly. Bernie Ryan had two young daughters of his own, one of whom was only months older than Laura.

There was, he would discover, a plausible explanation given for each of the deaths. Caleb had died at just 19 days old on 19 February 1989 from SIDS. His brother, Patrick, had died aged eight months on 13 February 1991 from a blockage of the airways due to an epileptic fit. Their sister Sarah died on 30 August 1993 aged 11 months, and the cause of her death was also recorded as SIDS. Craig told him that because of the deaths of Caleb, Patrick and Sarah they had been closely involved with Dr Chris Seton from the Westmead Children's Hospital in Sydney in order to remove the risk of it happening again with Laura. The detective stored the information away. Already something did not feel right to him about the little girl's death. But there was no mistaking her father's grief when Detective Ryan escorted him into the sterile room where Laura's tiny body was laid out so that she could be formally identified. The detective made a promise to himself that he would do everything he could to find out why the Folbigg children had died.

As the Folbiggs continued to mourn at the hospital, Detective Ryan drove over to their home in Millard Close where a police officer was on duty to preserve the integrity of the scene of the tragedy.

Detective Ryan observed that the house was clean and well kept. Conspicuously out of place was the paraphernalia left in the kitchen and near the break-fast bar by the ambulance crew in their haste to get Laura to hospital. He entered the room that bore Laura's name on a plaque on the door. Inside were the heartbreaking reminders of the little girl's life. Stuffed toys, a single bed in the far corner with pink sheets and a Wiggles doona cover and pillowcase. A second yellow-and-white pillowcase on the bed had four small circular stains. Detective Ryan made a note and had photographs taken.

He walked on into the lounge room, noting what he saw, unsure what could be important and what would be irrelevant to his investigation. On the futon in a corner of the lounge room he noted a pair of white Teletubby sandals and a baby's bottle. Near them was a baby monitor.

Detective Ryan had photographs taken of those as well, unaware at the time of just how important they would be in evaluating Kathleen Folbigg's version of Laura's last few minutes of life. With his inspection complete, Detective Ryan instructed the photographer on the items of interest. He then allowed the Folbiggs to return to their home and grieve in peace.

But Detective Ryan had not finished with the case by any stretch of the imagination. In the back of his mind he knew something was not right about the fact that four children from the same family had all died on separate occasions and in similar circumstances. The rookie detective, who had investigated a couple of murders but had never charged anyone with the actual crime, went away to contemplate the unthinkable. Was it possible? How could it have happened? Why had no one else questioned it? Where were the checks and balances to stop this from happening four times? Why had no one else spotted the clues? Was he the only one who thought the children could have been murdered? Could a mother really kill her children?

On that Monday afternoon Detective Ryan only had a suspicion and stood back to let the family grieve.

The following morning, Tuesday 2 March 1999, Craig and Kathleen Folbigg awoke to a world without children. Even the walls, where the day before pictures of Laura and her siblings had hung, were bare. Craig's despair was there for everyone to see. Kathy, by contrast, seemed emotionless. She telephoned their neighbour Deborah Grace who lived opposite. 'I've got some sad news to tell you. Laura has died.'

Mrs Grace was shocked. Only eight days before she had been with Kathy and Laura. The child had been a little grizzly, nothing out of the ordinary, and Kathy had been a little short with her. There had been no clue that something like this could have happened. 'How?' she asked.

'She died in her sleep,' said Kathy.

When Deborah Grace walked across the road she found both Kathy and Craig sitting outside the front of the house. Craig was crying uncontrollably. But Kathy was showing no emotion. Nothing at all. She was straight-faced; there were no tears in her eyes, no expression whatsoever.

Deborah Grace struggled for the right words. What could she, herself a mother, possibly say? What does anyone say when confronted with such a tragic loss – the death of an innocent child? 'How could this have happened?' she asked.

'Just like the rest of them,' was Kathy's chilling reply.

All that day friends and neighbours called with their condolences. Barbara Unicomb, who used to live in Millard Close, rushed around to the Folbiggs' house as soon as she heard the news. She had always remembered Kathy as a good mother. When she arrived Craig was still out the front of the house but Kathy had gone inside to the kitchen. Kathy was moving around the house and spared only brief moments from her chores to be with Barbara Unicomb. She supposed Kathy was upset, but her grief was not very obvious.

Everyone who visited the house that day clearly recalled later that Craig was distraught. The recollections of Kathy's emotional state varied. The neighbours who saw no emotion observed a different side of Kathy to the one she showed to her friends from the BodyFlex gymnasium. When Kathy's gym friends came to pay their respects they saw a very upset and grieving mother.

Gym instructor Jan Bull had been leading Kathy's fitness class on Monday. Kathy had told her that Laura had not seemed well and she would take her home for a nap rather than join Jan and Kerrie and her other gym friends for their usual morning tea. It was only a couple of hours later that the gym instructor received the phone call from Kathy informing her that Laura was dead. She and some other instructors from the gym were driving to Newcastle for a course at the time and so they did not visit Kathy until Tuesday morning. Jan later said she found Kathy to be as 'upset as any mother would be'. She told Kathy: 'Don't be a stranger to the gym. Come back even if you just want to have a cup of tea and the company. Come back as soon as you feel.'

Other gym friends were among the stream of people who came to offer their condolences on that bleak Tuesday. Housewife Debbie Goodchild recalled Kathy crying. 'She was devastated,' she said later. Judith Patterson, another gym friend and neighbour from the adjoining street who used to babysit Laura, also called around to the Folbiggs' house a couple of times that day. She later said that Kathy was hysterical. 'She was crying; shaking when she was crying. Sometimes she could hardly stand up because she was crying that much. She would settle down, like for a little while, like most people do, and then burst into tears, all right. It would only take a thought – and it would only take me saying something about Laura, or her thinking something and she would be just devastated.' Concerned for her grieving friend, Judith called around to the house every day until the funeral. Every day Kathy wept.

Craig would say later that the death of Laura had filled him with anger. 'I was devastated, but I recall mostly I was angry and I didn't know who to be angry at or why to be angry – other than not having her.' Craig's damning recollection was that his wife 'cried on cue'. She was only inconsolable when her friends were near.

Despite their different ways of dealing with their grief that week, the Folbiggs began what had become an all too familiar task and put in train arrangements for the funeral of yet another child.

Kathy's foster sister Lea Bown looked on little Laura as the granddaughter she had always wanted. On Monday 1 March, her husband's birthday, she had taken the call at her Melbourne home that had robbed her of that granddaughter forever. It was not the time to go into detail – she was told her sister had been sedated because of the distress. Instead she immediately got into the car with her daughter, Tanya, and drove for over 12 hours to Singleton. When she arrived, Kathy, in heartbreakingly poignant detail, described the day that Laura died. She recalled how at first she had decided not to go to the gym that day because Laura was off-colour. Then Laura perked up and told her mother that she wanted to go and play with her friends in the crèche and went to her bedroom to get the little bag she took with her. Kathy recounted all of the events of that final morning, including how she had found Laura not breathing and how she had called for help from Craig and the ambulance.

It was a tough week. Mrs Bown and her daughter stayed with Kathy and Craig in a bid to keep their spirits up. Kathy seemed very upset and wanted her sister there. Her moods fluctuated from despair to almost jovial at times. She confided to Lea that she felt very guilty that she had not gone into the bedroom to check on Laura sooner. Her pain was so intense that if she saw a baby in the street she would turn away. It was just too hard to bear. 'She would have her really down moments and have her up times as well before the funeral,' recalled Mrs Bown later.

There was a big turnout for the funeral. Kathy's friends were concerned for her. One of them, Debbie Goodchild, later recalled: 'She looked to me as if she had been sedated and she needed a helping hand to actually walk up the aisle to sit down for the service.' Sitting five rows behind the Folbiggs, gym instructor Jan Bull watched her friend's shoulders shake as she sobbed. 'Every now and then I would look at her and Craig. I noticed at one stage, I think she put her hand on Craig's back or sort of made like a comforting move towards Craig and then another time – a couple of times – I noticed the shoulders slumping down.' Afterwards she, like the other mourners, spoke to Kathy before heading back to Millard Close for the wake. She later related how Kathy appeared to be 'obviously upset. She just looked like someone that was trying to keep it together, to try and get through the difficulty as best she could'.

After they had made it through the service and the mourners had expressed their condolences to the couple, Craig and Kathy walked back to the car with Lea Bown. Tanya got in the front with Craig, who was driving, while Kathy sat in the back in between Lea and Craig's brother Michael.

113

'Well, thank fuck that's over. Now I can get on with things,' said Kathy.

To her startled sister, Kathy seemed like a different person from that moment on.

Back at the house for the wake Kathy caught up with her gym friends. They stood in the kitchen and chatted as the food and drink were served. Judith Patterson thought Kathy had perked up a little since the funeral. When later recalling the wake, Judith said: 'We reminisced just about the little things that Laura had done in her short time, and just brought little smiles to our faces that we remembered such silly things at such a time.' Although her friend could see Kathy was still upset and had tears in her eyes, she was talking a little bit more than she had been at the church.

Watching from the wings, Lea Bown saw things differently. She was still reeling from the comment in the car and Kathy's transformation from a weeping wreck to a totally different person. As she looked at her sister laughing and joking with her friends she thought to herself that Kathy was really enjoying – no, loving – being the centre of attention and was having a really good time.

Meanwhile, Craig was overwhelmed by his emotions. At the time he thought Kathy's outburst in the car had simply meant she wanted to get on with things back at the house for the wake. Later he would come to realise she really did mean that she was glad the funeral of her fourth child was over so that she could get on with the things she wanted to do with her life – such as going to the gym.

Her behaviour at the wake was also not what he had expected. He was stunned by what he considered to be the inappropriate behaviour of his wife. He too noticed the time she spent laughing and joking with her friends. Filled with a sense of loss when he returned from the funeral, he had wandered through the house before migrating to the backyard pool area where most of his large family had congregated. Only days before Laura had been frolicking in that very pool.

Eventually he went back inside the house and found Kathy laughing and talking with the girls from the gym. When he later recalled Kathy's conversation with her friends he was still bitter. 'They were just talking about memories and stuff and part of those memories was about, like, us meeting and growing up, I guess, because I recall being made fun of over a white suit that I had owned once . . . I didn't really want to take much more of it, so I left them and sat in the lounge room with the old people.'

With the funeral out of the way, Kathy heeded the advice of her friend and fitness instructor Jan Bull and resumed classes at the gym. Kathy's friends came to collect her on Monday morning. Her daughter had been dead for exactly one week. Looking out of her window onto Millard Close, neighbour Melissa Smith noted Kathy's departure to the gym. She reflected that apart from the day after Laura's death, Kathy did not seem to have been affected by the death of Laura one little bit.

8

The Diaries

IF THE FOLBIGGS' MARRIAGE was in trouble before Laura died it became much, much worse afterwards. Kathy resumed her life and threw herself into the pursuit of fitness at the BodyFlex gym. After a few weeks she returned to work at Retravision, and she also started going out with her girlfriends again. It was as if Laura never was. Craig, however, struggled. He mourned terribly for his little girl. He tried to put on a brave face to avoid dragging Kathy down with him as he had when the other children had died. As time passed it became clear that his efforts were not working.

After three or four weeks Kathy confronted him about his dour, moping demeanour. By that time Craig was taking antidepressants to try to deal with his grief. Craig later described what Kathy said to him. 'She told me that I was going to dig a big black hole and bury myself in it and that she wasn't going to go with that or cope with that.' Of himself at that time he later explained: 'I was, I thought, trying to tough it out and brave it out but she told me that it wasn't acceptable to her that I would do that with my life.'

They had been through this before. When both Caleb and Patrick died Craig had wanted to talk with Kathy about the babies and the life they had shared. She had refused, despite repeated coaxing from Craig, to talk about their children. Instead he had been left to withdraw and grieve alone. Her stubborn refusal to discuss their shared past with their children had become a considerable source of tension in the relationship.

Even though Craig knew the marriage was more fragile than ever, the couple made one last-ditch effort to save it. They drove down to Melbourne to stay with Kathy's sister Lea, with whom they had spent many happy hours, including one Christmas, with Laura. Even there at Lea's place, with its joyful memories and associations, Craig could not shake his sense of loss. He spent time asking Lea's nephew if he would accept all of Laura's belongings; Craig simply could not bear to throw them out.

It was no use, the respite in Melbourne failed to alleviate Craig's depression, or repair any of the cracks in the marriage. Kathy made it clear she did not have the energy, strength or will to try to pull Craig out of his despair. When they got back to Singleton she told him the marriage was over. Of their break-up, Craig later explained: 'She said that she couldn't deal with her own grief and she certainly wasn't going to be prepared to carry me and let me pull her down and that she just wanted to only be concerned for herself and not have to be concerned for anybody else.'

It was now only six weeks since Laura had died. Kathy packed her bags and moved out to a flat she had found herself a few kilometres away on the other side of town.

This was a body blow to Craig. He had now not only lost his beloved 19-month-old daughter but her mother as well. His wife of 16 years and his only living link to Laura, her two brothers and sister was gone. Six weeks ago he had had a family. Now he had nothing except loneliness, despair and haunting memories in an empty house.

Craig Folbigg battled on alone. He still went to work. Despite his pain, every day he tried to carry on and create something good from his time. But while his despair was etched into every line of his face, Kathy was back to her normal self, smiling and going about her daily business with any pain she felt buried deep inside. It was as if Laura had never been.

Singleton is a small town with only a couple of main streets and a population of 22,000 people. It was inevitable that he would see Kathy, going to work, heading for an aerobics class, passing his car dealership and going out at night. It hurt Craig to see Kathy making a new life for herself without him. They talked sometimes but she showed no signs of wanting to reconcile. It seemed he was the only one feeling the emptiness from Laura's loss and from their marriage breakdown. He soldiered on and weeks later, early in May 1999, he got up one morning and decided it was time to get a grip on things and sort out the house. Tidy things up a bit. He had asked Kathy what she wanted done with the belongings that she had left in the house. She told him to throw anything of hers in the bin. Whatever was there she did not want. So Craig set to work. He sorted through cupboards and drawers. He found things her foster parents had given her. Personal items. Books that she had read. He decided to pack away the china-painting materials her foster mother had given her in case she wanted them one day. Craig opened up her bedside drawer and there, among the bobby pins and hair clips near an old book, lay Kathy's diary. He recognised it instantly because he remembered his wife diligently writing in it every night a couple of years earlier. Succumbing to human impulse, Craig did what any jilted lover in his position would have done – he sat down to read it.

That decision changed the course of his life. Nothing would ever be the same again. What that book contained tore the very fabric of his existence. The handwritten diary covered the time from June 1996 to June 1997 – before Laura was born but included the time that Kathy was pregnant with Laura. What it contained made him question everything he had ever believed.

Among the almost illegible, and often badly spelt personal ramblings about weight gain and day-to-day frustrations in Kathleen Folbigg's diary were entries that did not sit comfortably with Craig's own recollection of their life at that time together. Sitting there, alone in the broken home they had tried to build together, he read his wife's entry for the day of 18 June 1996, during the period when they had been trying to conceive their fourth child, Laura:

> I'm ready this time and I know I'll have help and support this time. When I think I'm going to lose control like last times I'll just hand baby over to someone else. Not feel totally alone. Getting back into my exercise after will help my state of mind and sleeping, wherever possible as well. I have learned my lesson this time.

The words 'lose control' and 'learned my lesson' stunned him. Craig read the entry for 22 June 1996:

> I watched a movie today about schizophrenia. Wonder if I have a mild curse of that? I change moods really quickly. In my most dangerous mood I'm not nice to be around and always want to be anywhere but where I am.

Flicking through a couple of pages he paused at the entry for 21 July 1996 and read:

Stressed a little now, probably because it will be a couple of more months before I'm pregnant. Pretty sure I'm not now. Having, or had, what I think is a period. God, I hope so, or these tablets will cause brain damage. Probably just deserts for me, considering, but not fair for Craig at all. I would feel like a failure and couldn't cope at all. Can't be dwelling on what ifs. I truly deserve anything life throws at me, so my philosophy is whatever happens happens and it's the way it shall be. I'm going to try my hardest this time. If anything does happen, I'll just leave and try to let Craig go in peace and start again. No I wouldn't. I'm not that brave. Really, I depend on people and other people's help too much.

What did she mean by '*just deserts for me*'? And why did she deserve anything life threw at her but think that the same would not be fair to him? Hadn't they both lost their children? More and more questions were flooding into Craig's mind and he was scared to think about the answers. He read on. For 25 July 1996, a day he had been away, she wrote:

Did miss him in bed though. Just the comfort that someone else was going to be there. Like, I know that it would be me who would hear a break-in first, not him, but at least if I screamed loud enough he'd hear me.

Well he knew that was true. Once he fell asleep nothing disturbed him until the following morning. He slept like a log. On and on he read – lingering on the entry of 26 August 1996:

> Went to clairvoyant last week. So did Craig. I always
> believe there is more going on than just human nature.
> I seem content now because I now know that even
> though I'm responsible it's all right. She accepts and
> is happy there. I've always felt her strongly and now
> I know why. She is with me. I think my mother is too.

Hang on – responsible? '*Even though I'm responsible it's all right.*' Surely that could not be their daughter Sarah she was writing about, could it? Craig felt nauseated but the diary was compelling and he continued reading. On 8 September 1996 Kathy had written:

> Feel now is the time for us to have another baby. Have
> finally realised it's the right time for me. I have Craig and
> he wants a child that I can give him and I have enough
> friends now not to lose it like before.

Lose it like *how* before? With a mounting sense of dread Craig next read Kathy's entry on 14 October 1996:

> Children thing still isn't happening. Thinking of forgetting
> the idea. Nature, fate and the man upstairs have decided I
> don't get a fourth chance and rightly so, I suppose. I would
> like to make all my mistakes and terrible thinking be

corrected and mean something though. Plus I'm ready to continue my family time now. Obviously I am my father's daughter. But I think losing my temper stage and being frustrated with everything has passed. I now just let things happen and go with the flow, an attitude I should have had with all my children. If given the chance, I'll have it with the next one.

What was he reading? Craig could not get his brain to grasp the full impact of her words. What had been her '*mistakes*' and '*terrible thinking*' that she had thought God would rightly not allow them to have a fourth child? Their other three children had died of natural causes, hadn't they? Hadn't they?

The next entry, two weeks later, on 30 October 1996, only created more questions in Craig's mind:

I worry that my next child will suffer my psychological mood swings like the others did. I pray I'm prepared and ready, mindwise, for this next one. Maybe nature has decided I never will be and it will never happen.

Kathy's entry of 4 December 1996, when she had already found out that she was pregnant with Laura, only added to Craig's doubts and suspicions:

I have and will change my attitude and try earnestly not to let anything stress me to the max . . . If I have a clingy baby, then so be it; a catnapper, so be it. That will be when I will ask for help and sleep whenever I can to keep myself in a decent mood. I know now that battling wills and sleep deprivation were the causes last time.

Craig had spent enough time with medical experts from the Westmead Children's Hospital to know that battling wills and sleep deprivation were not the causes of Sudden Infant Death Syndrome. On 1 January 1997 his wife had confided to her diary:

Another year gone and what a year to come. I have a baby on the way which means major personal sacrifice for both of us, but I feel confident about it all going well this time. I'm going to call for help this time and not attempt to do everything myself any more. I know that was the main reason for all my stress before and stress made me do terrible things. Had a talk to Craig while in the bath tonight, our favourite talking spot. Haven't really cleared anything, just told him how I feel and what vibes I'm receiving from him.

The vibes Craig was receiving from the diary were frightening. What '*terrible things*' had she done? His brain whirled as he read the entry for 14 January 1997:

Well, best go. Time to return to bed and see if I can get some sleep. I'm sure this is training for when the baby arrives. That's okay. I'm pretty sure this time I'll handle it better. Hope so.

But had Kathy handled things better this time around? Laura was dead and Craig knew there was no obvious cause. On 4 February 1997 she had written:

Still can't sleep. Seem to be thinking of Patrick and Sarah and Caleb. Makes me seriously wonder whether I'm stupid or doing the right thing by having this baby. My guilt for how responsible I feel for them all haunts me. My fear of it happening again haunts me. My fear of Craig and I surviving, if I did, haunts me as well. I wonder whether having this one wasn't just a determination on my behalf to get it right and not be defeated by my total inadequate feelings about myself. What sort of mother am I? I have been a terrible one, that's what it boils down to. That's how I feel and that is what I think I'm trying to conquer with this baby, to prove that there is nothing wrong with me. If other women can do it, so can I. Is that the wrong reason to have a baby? Yes, I think so, but it's too late to realise now. I'm sure with the support I'm going to ask for, I'll get through. What scares me most will be when I'm alone with baby. How do I overcome that? Defeat that?

Craig re-read this entry. She must have made a mistake when she was writing; otherwise, what did she mean when she wrote: '*if* I *did, haunts me as well*'? Surely it should have read: '*if* it *did*'. Why did she think she had been a terrible mother? The children had been well cared for and had not been physically abused. What the hell did it mean? Craig continued skimming through the diary and read Kathy's views about him from the entry of 17 February 1997:

> He should be for me, forever. Just because a baby is entering our lives makes no difference really. One day it will leave. The others did. But this one's not going in the same fashion. This time I'm prepared and know what signals to watch out for in myself, changes in mood etc. Help I will get, if need be.

Craig's mind could not take in all of this. He read the entry for 28 April 1997:

> I think this baby deserves everything I can give her, considering I really gave nothing to the others. I think even my feelings towards this one are already deeper. Shame, but that's the way it is. I think it's because I'm 30 now and time to settle and bring up a child. Obviously I wasn't ready before all that.

Was this the diary of a woman who was grieving over the senseless, incomprehensible deaths of her children? Who played no part in those deaths? Why did she continue to write as if her actions and mood were related to their deaths in some way? With Laura's death so recent and his feelings so raw, Craig did not know what to think.

There was more. On 16 May 1997 Kathy wrote about her friend and neighbour Melissa Smith:

> I think she will be a great help in preventing me from stressing out as much as I have done in the past. Night time and early mornings, such as these, will be the worst for me. That's when wishing someone else was awake with me will matter, purely because of what happened before. Craig says he will stress and worry, but he still seems to sleep okay every night and did with Sarah. I really needed him to take over from me. This time I've already decided if I ever feel that way again I'm going to wake him up.

Craig's mind flashed back to the night Sarah died, back to a question that he had buried deep in the back of his mind after her death. He remembered how he had woken in the middle of the night at 1.10am and seen that Kathy and Sarah were not in the room. The light had been shining under the door and he had gone back to sleep, assuming that Kathy was bottle-feeding the baby in the next room as usual. Twenty minutes later he had been woken up by Kathy's screams and had found Sarah dead in her bed at the foot of their own bed. Kathy had later told him she had woken up and gone to the toilet and then had come back to find Sarah dead. If this were true it meant that in the space of 20 minutes she had got Sarah back to sleep, gone back to bed herself, and then had risen again to go to the toilet. Something had always jarred with Kathy's account. Craig had always harboured a suspicion about that but it had been too difficult to try to think what it had meant and there seemed to have been nowhere to go with his dark questions. Any thoughts of pursuing them had been thwarted by Kathy's refusal to discuss the children after their deaths. It had been too horrible to contemplate. Now those suspicions came flooding back and this time they were not going away.

Craig thought he was going to be sick. Had his wife killed their children? The diary in his shaking hands continued in the same chatty tone, belying the horror contained in the entries. He closed the diary after reading her entry for 29 May 1997:

> Need new diary soon. I've actually nearly filled up this one. Think it has helped writing my thoughts and feelings down regularly. Felt as though it's become a friend that I can off-load on and it doesn't . . . answer me. That's the best thing. Laugh at stupid things I have written in the past, but they were important to me back then, as this is now.

Suddenly this book had become very important to Craig as well. For a long time after each of his children had died he had waited for people to say something to him that indicated they thought something suspicious might have been going on. To raise the question or voice the doubts and suspicions that he secretly harboured deep within his subconscious. No one did. People were always so kind and sensitive to parents obviously grieving over the loss of a dearly loved baby. Who would have walked up to him in his time of distress and said: 'Listen mate, do you reckon the missus did it then?' No one. Even if anyone had thought it they would have dismissed it; they would have berated themselves for even thinking it. Craig knew himself that he had kept his own suspicions suppressed.

Now, with the diary in hand, he had to confront his suspicions head-on. What those suspicions meant was sickening. Abhorrent. A mother – his wife – killing her own children. His children. If it were true, the ramifications were truly terrifying. It was too awful to contemplate. Who else would even be prepared to think the unthinkable?

Craig picked up the phone and called Detective Bernie Ryan.

9

Sweet Little Lies

FOR SEVERAL WEEKS SINCE the death of little Laura Folbigg, Detective Senior Constable Bernie Ryan had not only been thinking the unthinkable, he had been actively thinking of ways to prove it. Fifteen days after Laura's death the doctor who had been on duty that day had written to him and requested the death be treated as murder.

Dr Quang Tuan Au had spent many sleepless nights before writing the letter to the detective. He had seen Craig run into the hospital, calling for his daughter, throwing himself onto her body. The loss of the little girl and her father's obvious grief had broken the doctor's heart. He had checked the records and seen that Laura had been through a battery of tests before being taken off her Sudden Infant Death Syndrome monitor only weeks before her death. However, Dr Tuan Au knew this was not a SIDS death. He felt there were so many coincidences – all the children were healthy, had died while alone in their mother's care, and there had been no obvious cause of death. Most of the children had been outside the age range of SIDS death and the syndrome had been proven not to be genetically linked. Dr Tuan Au wrote of his suspicions to Detective Ryan.

In the meantime, Laura's body had been sent to pathologist Dr Allan Cala at the New South Wales Institute of Forensic Medicine in Glebe, Sydney, for the postmortem. Here was a man who would finally recognise the warning signs that had occurred and ask some difficult questions about how the toddler had died.

Dr Cala was brilliantly qualified to look at the 19-month-old little girl's death. He had conducted thousands of autopsies. These included autopsies on children who were suspected to have died from SIDS and children who authorities suspected had been smothered. Such was his expertise he had presented a paper on asphyxia to a conference of health professionals in Canberra. As a squadron leader in the Royal Australian Air Force Reserves he was accredited with the Australian Defence Forces as a forensic expert and as part of his role had been required to examine the bodies of plane-crash victims. As part of that work, in conjunction with the United Nations, he had also gone to East Timor to exhume and examine the bodies of murder victims. In short, he was not a man to leave any line of inquiry unexplored when examining the body of a child who had been apparently healthy for all of her brief life.

When he first came to examine Laura's body on 1 March 1999 Dr Cala knew a few basic details of her background. He had been given a bare outline of the circumstances surrounding each of the deaths of her three siblings, in addition to her own medical history. This included the initial diagnosis of central apnoea when she was just over a week old, and the subsequent monitoring for over a year that had revealed no significant sleep abnormalities. Dr Cala was also made aware of the cold and flu symptoms Laura had exhibited in the week before her death and that she had been given an antihistamine, Demazin, to treat it. He also knew that Laura had appeared to be healthy the day before she died and that her mother had found her dead in bed after a morning nap. Armed with this information, he conducted a post-mortem examination of Laura's body.

It was not what he found that gave him the greatest cause for concern but what he did not find. There was no cause of death.

Dr Cala's examination revealed three old bruises on her legs, which were entirely normal for a child of her age, and lividity caused by the normal pooling of blood after death. He also found mild inflammation around the lining of Laura's heart – a condition known as myocarditis. The inflammation was consistent with the after-effects of flu and Dr Cala believed it played no part in her death. He examined her cardiovascular system, respiratory system, gastrointestinal system, kidney, spleen, heart, blood, lungs, did a full body X-ray and tested for poisons.

The only significant abnormalities were focally hae-morrhagic and collapsed lungs. In other words, Laura's lungs had collapsed and bled slightly either when she asphyxiated or during the attempts to resuscitate her.

The autopsy on Laura's sister, Sarah, had produced similar findings. But unlike Dr Hilton, who had recorded that Sarah had died from SIDS, Dr Cala's finding was that the blood in Laura's lungs offered no clues to be able to differentiate between whether she had died from SIDS, or, more sinisterly, whether she had been smothered.

Later, Dr Cala spoke of the difficulties of being able to distinguish between SIDS and deliberate smothering as causes of death. He recalled an autopsy he had performed on a six-month-old girl who had been found dead in her cot one morning. He found no evidence of bleeding in the lungs or marks on her face. 'It was only later that more accurate information came to light, and that information was given to me after I had done my post-mortem examination on that child where I found nothing at all, and I was given the information that the child had been deliberately smothered.

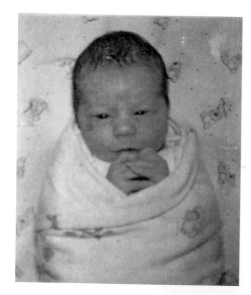

Caleb Gibson Folbigg was born on 1 February 1989. Caleb was well cared for and appeared to be thriving for the 19 days of his short life until his mother, Kathleen, claimed she found him lifeless in his cot. Doctors initially attributed his death to SIDS.

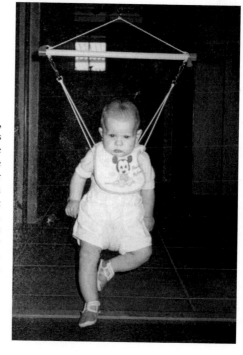

Patrick Allen Folbigg, born on 3 June 1990, was extremely healthy until he was rushed to hospital at the age of four months after Kathleen 'found' him in the middle of the night struggling to breathe. Ambulance officers saved his life but he suffered epilepsy and blindness until his death at the age of nine months of asphyxia, apparently suffered as the result of an epileptic seizure. This medical opinion was later revised.

Kathleen Folbigg nicknamed her third child, Sarah, 'the catnapper' because of her fitful sleeping patterns. Sarah died in the middle of the night of 30 August 1993 at the age of 10 months. SIDS was initially deemed to be the cause.

In the middle of the night that Sarah died, Craig woke up and noticed the time on the bedside clock was 1.10am. He saw that his wife and daughter were not in the bedroom. He fell back to sleep but was aware of Kathleen returning to bed. Twenty minutes later she raised the alarm that Sarah wasn't breathing. The Crown prosecutor, Mark Tedeschi QC, later asked why it was that Kathleen had written on the household calendar: 'Sarah left us at 1am'.

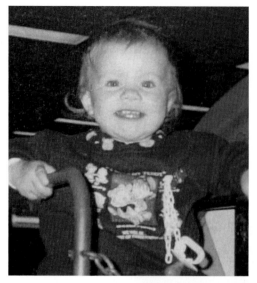

Laura Elizabeth Folbigg, born on 7 August 1997, was a healthy, well-behaved baby and Kathleen wrote in her diary soon after her new baby was born that she felt maternal instinct for the first time. Laura's sleeping and breathing patterns were carefully monitored for the first year of her life and she was found to be normal. Kathleen, however, was becoming increasingly frustrated with her marriage and motherhood.

Detective Bernie Ryan noted the heartbreaking reminders of a little girl's life when he examined the bedroom where 19-month-old Laura died on 1 March 1999, less than an hour after the toddler and Kathleen had returned home from visiting Craig at work.

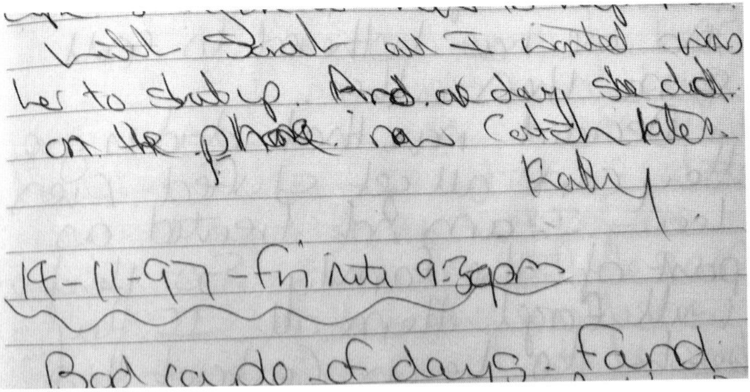

[handwritten text at top of page:]

...with Sarah all I wanted was her to shut up. And one day she did. on the phone. now catch later. Kathy

14-11-97 -Fri nite 9:30pm

Bad cpl of days. Fand

Several weeks after Laura's death, while sorting through his wife's bedside drawer, Craig found a diary. His decision to read it completely changed the course of their lives. He read many entries that made him doubt Kathleen, such as this one: 'With Sarah all I wanted was her to shut up. And one day she did.'

It was not long before Detective Bernie Ryan (pictured) wondered why no one had questioned why four children from the same family had all died in similar circumstances on separate occasions. Kathleen's diary confirmed his suspicions that the children had been smothered.

MOTHER STABBED

A MAN was seen to fatally stab a woman, Glebe Court was told today.

Thomas John Britton, 45, hoist driver, of Darvall Street, Balmain, was charged with the murder of Kathleen Mary Donavan at Annandale yesterday.

Prosecutor, Sgt. E. R. Briddick, said Britton had been living with Donavan.

She had an 18-months-old child.

Sgt. Briddick said that in the past few months, Donavan had left Britton.

Britton, he said, had been seen at Donavan's place yesterday.

"He was seen delivering a stab blow to the woman," Sgt. Briddick said.

Britton waited until police arrived at the scene, he said.

Mr A. Chick, S.M., remanded Britton to the Coroner's Court on December 18 and refused bail.

Kathleen's early years were very traumatic. In 1968, when she was 18 months old, her father, Thomas 'Jack' Britton, stabbed her mother, Kathleen Donavan, to death. Kathleen was then fostered out to the Marlborough family and grew up in Newcastle, never having contact with her father again.

Britton was sentenced to life imprisonment for the murder of his de facto wife. After serving 14 years of his jail term, he was deported back to his home town in Wales. Kathleen continued to wonder about him and she wrote in her diary in 1996: 'Obviously I am my father's daughter' when describing her temper and the frustration she felt with her first three children. Britton died in 1999.

When Kathleen was charged with the murder of her four children, her boyfriend of 10 months, Tony Lambkin, was badly shaken up by her arrest. Tony was head over heels in love with Kathleen and hoped they would marry and have children together some day. He accompanied her to some initial court hearings but because of her public notoriety it was difficult for Kathleen to sustain the relationship and it ended after two years.

Kathleen's constant friend and confidante during the Supreme Court trial was Salvation Army court chaplain Major Joyce Harmer. In her role supporting people in distress, Major Harmer sat in court in the same place so Kathleen had a friendly face to turn to if she needed it.

Crown prosecutor Mark Tedeschi QC suggested Kathleen's possible motive for smothering each of her children: 'The accused had a very low threshold for stress and she was also deeply resentful at the intrusions that her children made on her own life and, in particular, on her sleep, her ability to go to the gym, and her ability to socialise . . . '

During the initial stages of police investigations into Kathleen, her foster sister, Lea Bown, felt that police were conducting a witch-hunt. Detective Ryan gradually convinced Lea that Kathleen had murdered her children. For at least a year before the trial, Lea recorded all of her phone conversations with her sister and reported them back to Detective Ryan.

Craig Folbigg's girlfriend, Helen Pearce, was stoic in her support for him during the Supreme Court trial where he gave evidence that helped convict his estranged wife.

After Kathleen was convicted of the manslaughter of Caleb, grievous bodily harm and the murder of Patrick, and the murders of Sarah and Laura, Craig read from a prepared statement to reporters outside the courthouse: 'My humble thanks go to 12 people I have never formally met who today share the honour of having set four beautiful souls free to rest in peace.'

Every day of the trial, Kathleen appeared immaculately dressed and coiffured, betraying no sign of what was happening inside. After the guilty verdicts were delivered, Kathleen sobbed uncontrollably. What madness had caused her to murder her children? Detective Ryan had pondered her state of mind for some time and concluded: 'She wasn't mad, just bad.'

'In short one of the caregivers had confessed to another person that they had deliberately smothered the child. There was nothing except that admission to distinguish it at the time of my examination, or later, from SIDS and deliberate smothering.'

Now he had another child on the mortuary slab with no obvious cause of death. Dr Cala's suspicions were aroused. Over the course of the next couple of days he went back to Laura's body three times to examine her face closely for any sign of smothering. He checked for any slight bruising that might show through in the days after death. Dr Cala found nothing. He then conducted a facial dissection to look for tiny injuries beneath the skin. Again he drew a blank. This was not surprising. Later he spoke of this finding, reporting, 'There are generally no positive signs of suffocation, so in essence you can almost never rule it out'.

Rather than record a verdict of SIDS as Professor Hilton had done in the case of Sarah Folbigg, Dr Cala gave the cause of death as undetermined and later explained this finding in court: 'Undetermined causes of death include natural causes of death that are unable to be found and other inflicted causes of death such as suffocation, accidental causes of death and so on . . . as opposed to SIDS, which is quite different. SIDS is, I have to say, not a natural disease; it is an invented term. It stands for, of course, Sudden Infant Death Syndrome, and it was invented about 30 years ago to try to come to an understanding about cot death and who died and under what circumstances . . . SIDS is thought to be due to some natural process. It is not known what it is. But after a post-mortem examination and examination of the scene . . . where the child died, after microbiological testing and toxicological testing and so on, [if] no cause of death is able to be established it's felt then that the child has died of SIDS.'

Dr Cala felt very confident that Laura had not died from a natural process that could be attributed to SIDS. 'Firstly Laura Folbigg was about 20 months old when she died . . . to classify a death as SIDS it generally falls within the age of about three to six months of age. So she is clearly three times over the age for that and that by itself . . . is a very important thing to consider. In my opinion [that] would categorically exclude this child's death as being due to SIDS, irrespective of any family history of other deaths and so on. In isolation this would not and should not be called SIDS.'

There was another common factor in SIDS deaths that did not appear to apply to Laura. SIDS children are normally found the following morning, hours after they have been fed in the middle of the night. Laura and all the other Folbigg children had been found by their mother just moments after she had attended to them.

Dr Cala voiced his concerns to Detective Bernie Ryan. The detective, already very concerned about the inconsistencies he was finding in the sequence of events as explained to him by the child's parents, asked Dr Cala to look into all four deaths. He wanted a medical overview to find out if what he thought had happened to Laura had happened to all of the Folbigg children.

The pathologist obliged. He took his own examination of Laura as well as the medical histories, hospital and GP visits and post-mortem reports of Caleb, Patrick and Sarah, and applied them to the American Academy of Paediatrics criteria on distinguishing SIDS from fatal child-abuse cases. Dr Cala, together with the majority of the international medical community, agreed with the guidelines.

Essentially the American criteria defined SIDS, or cot death, as the sudden death of a child that could not be explained by a review of the child's medical history, an autopsy or an examination of the place where the child died. It said SIDS was most common in babies between the ages of one and six months with almost all SIDS cases happening before the baby reached six months of age.

The criteria also described the warning signs that indicate a child may have been suffocated:

It is impossible to distinguish at autopsy between SIDS and accidental or deliberate asphyxiation with a soft object. However, certain circumstances should indicate the possibility of intentional suffocation including:

- *Previous recurrent cyanosis (bluing of the lips and fingers), apnoea (cessation of breathing) or Acute Life Threatening Event [ALTE] while in the care of the same person.*
- *Previous unexpected or unexplained deaths of one or more siblings.*
- *Simultaneous or nearly simultaneous death of twins.*
- *Previous death of infants under the care of the same unrelated person.*
- *Discovery of blood on the infant's nose or mouth in association with ALTEs.*

Armed with this information and the Folbigg children's medical records, Dr Cala went back to Detective Ryan with some very disturbing conclusions drawn purely from the medical evidence.

He began with Caleb Folbigg. Firstly, he told the detective he had never in his experience or his wide reading of medical literature or even in discussion with colleagues, known of a child to die from a floppy larynx. Caleb was younger than the one month that the guidelines indicated SIDS commonly started from. If Dr Cala had conducted the post-mortem on Caleb he would have diagnosed the cause of death as 'undetermined'. Caleb's death was consistent with him being deliberately suffocated. There was no other explanation for his death. Dr Cala told the policeman that he did not agree with the original diagnosis that Caleb had died from SIDS.

Referring to the American Academy of Paediatrics document, he told Detective Ryan that Patrick's acute life-threatening event (ALTE) was also consistent with him having been smothered. If he had conducted the post-mortem on Patrick he would have borne that in mind when examining Patrick's body. He would not have looked at epilepsy as a cause of death but simply diagnosed it again as 'undetermined'. The autopsy results contained none of the clues he would have expected for a child's death from natural causes. Patrick was outside the guidelines' six-month usual age limit for SIDS. It was hard to prove, but Dr Cala was suspicious about Patrick's cause of death.

With Sarah, alarm bells were really ringing for Dr Cala. Firstly, if he had carried out the post-mortem he would have taken photographs of the two tiny puncture marks on Sarah's chin. 'I think any injury on the face of a child whose death you are asked to examine, and obviously perform a post-mortem examination, should make one cautious and therefore I think that for the purposes of collecting good evidence to use later in formulating a cause of death . . . it is a good practice to take photographic pictures of injuries. Particularly, as I say, around the face of a child.' He also said that he did not think the marks were caused by attempts to resuscitate Sarah. 'I have seen a lot of children who have been resuscitated successfully and unsuccessfully and most don't have marks on their faces.' He was convinced that an oxygen mask certainly would not have caused the two tiny puncture marks because it was his opinion that because masks are very soft around the edges they do not cause abrasions. Then there was Sarah's age. 'SIDS deaths are generally around three to six months of age, and much older than that I think you should be looking seriously at other diagnoses rather than SIDS. And certainly beyond 12 months old I would say categorically exclude it . . . Sarah was . . . approaching 12 months of age, so that alone would make me hesitant to call this case SIDS.'

Dr Cala told Detective Ryan that again the cause of death should have been recorded as undetermined. Sarah, in his opinion, probably died from an acute asphyxiating event of unknown causes – consistent with her being smothered.

Three of the children were older than the custom-ary six-month limit for SIDS, they were found by their mother almost immediately after they had stopped breathing, their autopsies provided no real clues as to their cause of death, and examination of the area where each child had died also drew a blank.

'If you are seeking from me one global explanation to account for all four deaths rather than a diagnosis for each one which may be different from the other three, then I think that the diagnosis medically still remains – deliberate smothering,' Dr Cala told the detective.

That was the medical evidence in medical terminology. In Detective Ryan's language it told him what he had suspected – Caleb, Patrick, Sarah and Laura had all been murdered. Now the policeman had to gather evidence to show who did it.

After Dr Cala told him that he believed all four of the Folbigg babies had been smothered, Detective Ryan set to work with a vengeance. The thing that he could not shake from his mind was the image of little Laura Folbigg's face when he had seen her body in the hospital. It made him think of his own daughter of a similar age. He simply could not let her death go unavenged. He could not allow her killer to walk free.

There was plenty to be suspicious about and a lot of unhappy coincidences. Detective Ryan had four bodies on his hands. Four innocent victims who seemed to have no medical reason to die. They had been perfectly healthy. The policeman was looking at the work of a serial killer. But there were still no hard facts – no murder weapon, no confession, no obvious clues – for the policeman to work on. Together with his colleagues, police officers Mick Prentice, Dave Frith and Bob Wells, and support officer Carina Murray, he began by digging up every document relating to the medical history and autopsies of the Folbigg children. The police officers collected tissue samples that had been kept on the medical files of all four babies for further testing. For hours and hours they scoured the internet for similar cases and expert opinions. Quickly the case file filled dozens of folders and involved thousands of pieces of paper.

In the middle of it all Detective Ryan received a phone call from Craig Folbigg. This was the breakthrough Detective Ryan had been hoping for. Craig wanted to see him. He had found something that had sent a lot of doubts and fears running through his head.

It was Wednesday night, 14 May 1999, when Detective Ryan visited Craig Folbigg at home in Millard Close, Singleton. The detective, already aware that Kathy had moved out, was greeted at the front door by Craig, who had a friend with him at the house for support. Detective Ryan sat down and listened at length to the bereaved father's thoughts and fears about the deaths of his children. Craig pointed out the inconsistencies in Kathy's description of the events on the day of Laura's death. Why, he asked, were the Teletubby shoes on the futon with a bottle if Kathy had taken them off in the hallway while she carried the sleeping child to bed as she had claimed? Why was the monitor still plugged into the wall if Kathy had been listening to it as she hung out the washing? Craig went on to explain his doubts surrounding Sarah's death – how she had not been in her bed just 20 minutes before his wife claimed to have found her, warm to the touch but not breathing. Crucially, he told Detective Ryan about the diary he had found and what it contained. Reading Kathy's innermost thoughts had suddenly made sense out of a lot of strange things in his life. The disquieting kind of sense that perhaps only a policeman would understand, and that is why he had decided to call Detective Ryan.

Craig showed the young detective the diary. It only took a few moments for Detective Ryan to realise he had found the smoking gun; the vital piece of evidence that revealed the hand of the killer. He arranged for Craig to bring the diary to Singleton Police Station and make a statement.

Five days later, on 19 May, Craig did exactly that. Although he was apprehensive about the interview he felt it was important to explain to the police the concerns he had that had been compounded by what he had read in his wife's diary. He felt it was an obligation he owed his children.

Detective Ryan conducted the interview by the book. He made Craig as comfortable as possible under the circumstances and then began asking him questions to help give a free-flowing account for the record. 'Just tell me word for word what life was like. What did you live like? What did the babies live like?'

the detective asked. He sat at the computer typing up the statement as Craig answered the many questions about his everyday life with Kathy, and about the relationship between Kathy and the children. He handed over the diary he had found, as well as his old 1989 work diary, which Kathy had taken and used for herself.

Craig was nervous. He was concerned about the ramifications of what he was telling the police officer about his wife. His nerves made him talkative. Although Detective Ryan kept things very casual and comfortable, it remained a fairly stressful day and Craig was not sure what or what not to tell the detective. As it happened he did not have time to finish the statement that day and they stopped before reaching the details of Sarah's death and whether she had been in bed or not when Craig had woken up 20 minutes before Kathy raised the alarm.

As Craig had already missed a day of work giving the first part of his police statement, it was arranged that he would return and complete the statement four days later on Sunday 23 May. It would prove a difficult day for both Craig Folbigg and Bernie Ryan.

The night before he was due to return to Singleton Police Station, Craig bought some takeaway food and ate it in the car as he drove over to Kathy's flat. She was getting ready to go out to a ball. They chatted but he did not mention his visit to the police or the arrangement he had made with Detective Ryan for the next day.

Craig still loved his wife. He remained besotted by her. Kathy's magnetic power over men still held him in its thrall. That night he sat outside in his car, waiting for her to return to her flat. She came back with an American businessman she had met at the gym. They stopped outside and began kissing on the veranda. Once they had gone inside, Craig could see that they were undressing each other in the lounge room. He sat crying on the steps before getting back in his car and driving away. However, the pain of seeing his wife with another man was too much for him to bear. In a tumult of emotion he turned the car around and drove back to her flat to confront Kathy. He stormed back up the steps and banged angrily on the door.

'Why did my daughter have to die for you to achieve all this?' he screamed.

Kathy flung the door open. 'You're an arsehole!' she spat, and then slammed the door in his face.

Craig stood staring blankly at the door before turning on his heel, returning to the car and driving home. He had only just let himself in and begun to settle his still very shaken nerves when Kathy came screaming up the driveway.

She was furious. 'Where do you get off on accusing me of Laura's death?'

'Look, I'm not the only one that thinks you did it,' said Craig.

'Who else?' demanded Kathy.

'The police and more than likely a lot of other people around town.'

Kathy swore.

'Well it just doesn't add up,' said Craig.

Kathy, inside the house by now, sank onto the lounge and burst into tears. 'How could you think that of me? I was their mother, I loved them.'

Hearing these words, Craig's heart broke. Softened and upset by the exchange, Craig told her that he had been to the police a few days earlier. 'I found your diary. Had some pretty horrible things written in it and I gave it to Bernie.'

'What do you mean? What's written in it?' asked Kathy.

'Oh, there was that thing about being your father's daughter . . .' Craig began.

From that moment Kathy's attitude changed and she became friendlier. 'How could you say those things about me? You know I loved them.'

For once she was happy to start discussing their life and parenting together. The more they talked the more Craig felt terrible for going to the police with his suspicions about his wife. He felt like a mongrel.

'You've got to tell them the truth. You've got to tell them. You know I loved those kids,' Kathy urged. She

146

asked Craig to go back on Sunday and tell the truth. Craig understood what she meant – her own version of the truth. But Kathy appeared happy to get back together and indicated as much. Craig so badly wanted to reconcile. He loved her after all.

After Kathy left the house Craig thought about what she had said. She was right. He had really seen how she had loved their kids. He would have to make it right. A couple of years later he recalled how he tried to rectify his statement in accordance with Kathy's wishes. 'So when I went back to Bernie, I asked him to rewind back through his machine, and told him what I wanted him to change.'

Craig went on to soften some of the things he had told the detective on their first meeting at Millard Close by giving a revised statement.

Detective Ryan was not convinced by Craig's new statement. Knowing that his revisions were not the truth, Craig could not even bear to read the front of the statement he signed which read:

This statement made by me accurately sets out the evidence which I would be prepared, if necessary, to give in court as a witness. The statement is true to the best of my knowledge and belief and I make it knowing that if it is tendered in evidence I shall be liable for prosecution if I have wilfully stated in it anything which I know to be false or do not believe to be true.

Craig later described that statement as something he had put at the bottom of his budgie cage. He did not like signing it. On that Sunday though it did not matter. He was back with Kathy. He loved her. Within a month she had moved back into their family home.

10

I am my Father's Daughter

FOR A WHILE IT WAS like dating again. Kathy would go up to the house or Craig would call on her at the flat and they would spend the evening together talking and having dinner. They reminisced, remembering the good times when they had first met, before they had children.

Craig was still so besotted by his wife that he succeeded for a while in suppressing the doubts he had about her in relation to the children. Certain phrases from her diary entries would pop into his mind when he was least expecting it, particularly the phrase 'Obviously I am my father's daughter' she had used when describing the way she had lost her temper when frustrated with her children.

The fact that she had compared herself to her father had horrifying implications that he preferred not to contemplate. Instead he chose to focus on rebuilding his marriage with the woman he had loved for almost 15 years.

Craig was well aware of the dark history of Kathy's

biological parents and of her early childhood. Kathy had been fostered as a three-year-old by Neville and Deirdre Marlborough. At the time, her foster sister, Lea, was 15 and thrilled to have a baby sister. When speaking of her sister Lea said in 2003: 'She was an adorable child; we all loved her to bits.' Deirdre Marlborough recalled her foster daughter as a 'very pretty little girl with really blonde curly hair' and said that growing up Kathy had been a 'most attractive' child who turned into 'a normal teenager'.

Kathy fulfilled her foster parents need for another child. Their own two children had grown up but Deirdre and Neville Marlborough loved children and yearned for more. 'We used to take [in] children from church homes; both of us loved kids, and we just wanted another,' said Mrs Marlborough. 'We couldn't adopt any of the church kids and Kathy came to us through the government.' Her foster family loved Kathy and included her in everything they did, including several overseas holidays to Malaysia, the United States and Canada, in addition to family holidays around Australia.

Kathy had always been curious about her natural family. She would later tell Detective Bernie Ryan that her questions to the Marlboroughs about her biological parents resulted in 'brick walls in my face' as her foster family did not want her asking too many difficult questions about her past. As a teenager Kathy finally managed to track down and meet her natural mother's brother who told her that her father had killed her mother. However, he did not go into much more detail. This simply aroused more curiosity in Kathy about her parents and after she had met Craig and settled down with her new husband he encouraged her to find out more. She tracked down two half-sisters in Queensland and two aunts, one in Queensland and one in Windsor, in the outer suburbs of Sydney. She made contact with them by letter and by phone. Over the years she began to meet her family members and the detail of what happened to her parents began to be filled in. The search for the truth went on over many years.

It was on her 32nd birthday in 1999 that Kathy and Craig went to meet her family in Windsor while some of the Queensland relatives were visiting and the full, complete and painful truth of what had happened was finally revealed to her. She met an uncle there who had looked after her for a while before she was placed in an orphanage and eventually fostered to the Marlboroughs. Her uncle told her that her natural family had hidden her from her father 'because he turned out to be not a very nice sort of a man'. In fact, with her mother dead and her father in jail for her murder there was no one who wanted little Kathleen. It was painful for the family to meet her now, at her insistence, and revisit the painful past. And it was painful for one very good reason. Kathy's father, Thomas John Britton, was a very bad man.

Britton had been born in Wales, one of 10 children, and went to sea young. Even at that age he had a reputation for being quick with his fists and good with the ladies. He liked a drink as well. Britton jumped ship in Australia in the post-war years and started work on road-making crews before becoming a hoist driver at Sydney's Balmain docks. One anonymous former friend told a Sydney newspaper years later that he was a knockabout guy with a vicious streak, particularly with women. He said Britton had lost his job at a cement plant because he grabbed his leading hand by the throat. Apparently in another job he hit a blacksmith in the face with a 7lb (3.1kg) hammer. Britton was certainly tough and supplemented his income as a hitman and debt collector for notorious underworld figures Robert Trimbole and Lenny McPherson. When people could not pay, Thomas 'Jack' Britton really earnt his money – he would rough up people – break their legs or kneecap them.

When he had first arrived in Sydney Britton had married nurse Margaret Cope. They lived in Railway Avenue, East Portland, in western Sydney, and had a son – Kathleen Folbigg's half-brother. That period of stability did not last long. In 1952 he slashed Margaret Cope's throat with a knife. She survived and Britton served eight months in jail for inflicting grievous bodily harm. He fathered several other children before falling for the charms of Kathy's mother, Kathleen Donavan. Whatever his skill as a ladies' man, the effect lasted less than three years on Kathleen Donavan. In November 1968 the 39-year-old factory worker walked out on him and their baby daughter, Kathy. A gambler and drinker, it was par for the course for her – she had abandoned a previous husband with their daughter and adopted son.

Forty-five-year-old Britton suspected Kathleen Donavan was cheating on him. In the police statement he later gave, Britton said she had left him with the baby during a family picnic at Nielsen Park, Vaucluse, on 24 November 1968. 'I objected to her drinking so much with the child present. She told me she would drink what she liked, when she liked and with whom she liked,' Britton said.

'She then drank one beer quick and went to drink another one. I took it from her and put it on the table. She just grabbed her bag and went. She left the child with me. She had my week's wages in her bag, about $70.'

Broke, Britton took baby Kathy back on the ferry across the harbour to Drummoyne Wharf and then carried her and their two bags of picnic things to their home in Darvall Street, Balmain.

Meanwhile, after storming off, Kathleen had gone to stay with her friends Vince and Moya O'Brien in

Pritchard Street, Annandale. Moya O'Brien knew her friend Kathleen was in trouble. Kathleen had told her that every morning Britton would hold a knife to her throat and ask: 'Will I or won't I?' Thirty-five years later Moya O'Brien recalled: 'She came knocking on our door, but she was definitely not drunk; she was in a tizz. Her intention was to get that little child back. She should have run and run and run, but I know she didn't want to leave that baby. She was sincere. She opened a bank account; she made one deposit before she died. That baby was mother's little girl. Her mum used to carry her around everywhere on her hip. I think everyone should know that she was a good mother . . . Her father was the monster.'

Back in Balmain, baby Kathy was fretting for her mother. Britton tracked Kathleen Donavan down to the house in Annandale and knocked on the door. 'I begged and pleaded with her to come back to me and the child. She refused point-blank. She said she didn't want anything to do with me or the baby,' he later said. 'It was from then that it all started to boil up inside me. I gave her a smack in the mouth.'

Britton needed money so he took baby Kathy to be cared for in the Glebe home of his friend Charles Budden and his wife while he went back to work on the docks. Kathleen Donavan was constantly on his mind. A few days later he was travelling on the bus when he saw her in a Balmain street. He jumped off and again begged her to come home. When that did not work he threatened to report her to the social services. He later said she told him 'she could not care less and was not coming home'. They started arguing about her blowing his $70 at the bookies and Kathleen retreated into a butcher's shop. Britton followed her inside and punched her in the face.

Britton considered himself a reasonably good drinker and on the night of 8 December 1968 sank 14 to 16 middies of beer before finding himself again outside the Pritchard Street home in Annandale where Kathleen Donavan was staying. When she arrived home in a taxi, Britton approached her. He later gave an account of their conversation. 'I could see she had been drinking. I then asked her again would she consider coming back home. I told her the baby was fretting for her and not eating. She said she couldn't care less and she was not coming home.'

Neighbours heard them arguing. Moya O'Brien later reported she heard him tell Kathleen: 'You are a black slut for leaving an 18-month-old baby. I'll stick a knife in your ribs.'

Britton stabbed Kathleen 24 times with a 25cm-long carving knife. She died in the street. Later he spoke of his crime: 'I done what I done. Then I threw the knife on to the footpath. I couldn't realise that she was dead. I kissed her and cradled her in my arms. I then told two people to ring the police as I thought

I had done my wife some harm. I just waited there until the police arrived. When she was on the ground I rearranged her clothes as I did not want anyone to see her like that. The bloke upstairs told me to get away from her and I told him to get to buggery.'

Neighbour Elizabeth Lorik said at the time that she heard the couple fighting she went out to her front garden to investigate. 'I saw a man with a knife in his right hand. I saw him push the knife into her left breast. He dropped the knife, and then he bent down and pulled her dress down because it had been caught up. The man looked up and asked me: "Will somebody ring the police?"

'I said: "We already did".

'He said: "I had to kill her because she'd kill my child." '

She then saw Britton kneel beside the woman, kiss her and say 'I'm sorry I had to do it'.

Britton was tried and found guilty of murdering his de facto wife Kathleen Donavan. On 26 May 1969 Mr Justice Le Gay Brereton sentenced him to life imprisonment. He served 14 years in prison and was then deported. Britton returned to Pontypool, his home village in Wales – still home to many of his siblings and their families – where he lied about his time in Australia.

Britton's first child, a son now in his 50s, had very little to do with him when he returned but a nephew, Roger Brandon, and Roger's wife, Margaret, did have contact with him. He never told them about his daughter Kathleen.

In fact, Kathleen Folbigg did not know of her father's whereabouts until his family was tracked down by *The Australian* newspaper when her own trial hit national and international headlines. By then Jack Britton was already dead. Mr Brandon told the newspaper: 'Jack never really opened up about his time in Australia so we never really knew what happened to him out there.'

He knew his uncle had served a jail term in Australia but the details of the reason for this remained hazy. 'He said he had killed an Italian man in self-defence and it had something to do with Australian crime gangs,' said Mr Britton.

The locals at Britton's regular drinking haunt, the White Hart, knew to steer well clear of him. Even in old age he had been known to successfully take on bigger men 50 years his junior. 'He was not a big guy but he was a tough old fellow with a real fiery temper,' said Mr Brandon.

Peter Bevan, White Hart publican, knew Britton well. 'He was in here every afternoon and every night. Jack could be happy enough but he could also be bloody cantankerous. We all knew he did time in Australia but he told me he had caught a bloke in bed with his wife and killed him on the spot.'

Another drinker claimed: 'He told me it was some

guy who had been on with his wife but he said he killed him in a pub.'

Britton celebrated his 75th birthday in October 1998 and then his health deteriorated. On the evening of 23 February 1999 Mr Brandon called in to check on Britton at his flat and found him dead in the chair at the kitchen table, with his evening meal half ready. Brandon's wife, Margaret, had been the last person to see him alive when she popped in to see him that morning.

Mr Brandon set about going through Britton's personal effects. In one box he found a well-worn envelope containing a lock of hair – the fine curly golden-red hair of a young child. 'Jack did mumble something once about having the hair of a daughter or granddaughter but it never made any sense because we didn't know about any daughter,' said Mr Brandon later.

Kathleen Folbigg's no-good father had kept a lock of her baby hair until the day he died, six days before his baby granddaughter, Laura Folbigg, would die on the other side of the world.

Kathy had only been 18 months old when her father had murdered her mother with a carving knife and could remember nothing about the killing or her parents. After reading her own Department of

Community Services files and finding out stories from her natural family about her mother and father, she felt her father had wasted his life, and her mother had not been much better – Kathy realised she had been a drunk and a gambler and had often left her baby daughter in the care of others.

Craig knew that when Kathy had written in her diary on 14 October 1996 the words 'Obviously I am my father's daughter' she had already known a great deal about the man who had killed her mother. After Craig had read her diary, she told him that the diary entry simply meant that in her eyes her father was a loser and she was a loser as well. In the weeks following their reconciliation in May 1999, despite already having taken his suspicions about Kathy to the police, Craig wanted so much to believe that his wife was telling him the truth that he ignored any doubts that crept into his mind. He tried to make a new life for himself and the woman that he continued to love, the mother of his four dead children – a woman with a tragic past.

11
Odyssey

ONCE HE HAD READ Kathleen Folbigg's diary, Detective Ryan knew that he was now involved in a murder investigation. However, proving that Kathleen Folbigg had smothered her children was not going to be straightforward, despite the evidence of the diary and the medical opinion of Dr Quang Tuan Au and Dr Cala. Craig and Kathy had reunited and Craig had softened his evidence. There had been no admissions. This was not going to be an easy case.

Detective Ryan needed help. Expert help. He contacted Dr Susan Beal at the Women and Children's Hospital in Adelaide where she had been one of Australia's leading SIDS experts for over 30 years. She had been involved in a review of every sudden infant death in the state, over 500, since 1970. She explained to him the background of SIDS in Australia and how back in 1978 she had published her concerns about the contributing factors to SIDS. By that stage she had visited about 150 families and found two disturbing things: firstly that most babies had been found dead

160

facedown, lying on their stomachs; and secondly that others were found with bedclothes over their heads.

She had set about finding out what the community generally did with their children when they put them to bed. She found that 30 per cent of the community laid their babies on their stomachs. Significantly, 80 per cent of the children who died were sleeping on their stomachs. Dr Beal then set out to get other people overseas in the UK and New Zealand to do the same SIDS research that was being carried out in Australia. Ultimately it was decided that babies should not be placed on their stomachs and, as a result, the incidence of SIDS throughout the western world more than halved. As a result of that work, the 'Back to Sleep' campaign was launched in the early 1990s with dramatic success, SIDS dropping in Australia from 40 cases per year down to less than 10.

Detective Ryan asked Dr Beal to look at the medical evidence and histories he had gathered on each of the Folbigg children. With Caleb she said she would have given his cause of death as SIDS with two provisos: 'The normal age range [for SIDS deaths] is one to six months. So this child being under three weeks puts it in a slightly different category. And this child being supine, lying on its back . . . both of which make SIDS less likely but don't exclude it.' The death was, she thought, consistent with Caleb being smothered by an adult.

Looking at Patrick's records she said it was most unlikely that his first acute life-threatening event (ALTE) was caused by epilepsy. More likely it was the result of an acute asphyxiating event. 'Children who have epileptic fits at that young age usually have a disease process that causes the fit, and you usually can find that either on EEG or autopsy,' she said. The doctor's view was that he was smothered and that that was also the cause of his death.

Dr Beal then studied Sarah's death and found it was like Caleb's in that she was outside the usual age range for SIDS and was found on her back, not on her stomach. The displaced uvula had nothing to do with her death but had been displaced during the post-mortem. Her death was also consistent with deliberate smothering by an adult.

In Laura's case, Dr Beal advised Detective Ryan that no two pathologists would agree on the issue of myocarditis – inflammation of the heart. She said that she had heard of cases where children who died from drowning or even from swallowing a peanut were described by doctors as having died from myocarditis. Instead she felt Laura's death was also consistent with being deliberately smothered by an adult, as in the case of all her siblings. Dr Beal could not think of a natural cause to explain all four deaths.

Detective Ryan now had a world-respected SIDS expert who agreed with his own beliefs. He went to

Canberra and consulted Dr Peter Herdson, the head pathologist for the Australian Capital Territory, at the Royal Canberra Hospital. Detective Ryan once again produced the medical details on the four children.

Dr Herdson told him that it was extremely difficult to distinguish between accidental and deliberate suffocation. 'In my experience it would be virtually impossible. In both instances, there may be virtually nothing defined. It is obvious that in some circumstances of suffocation there are marks, or the circumstances, for example, of a body getting wedged into the bottom of the bed or into the back of a sofa; it is those sorts of things which can help you in coming to a diagnosis of suffocation.'

The one thing he could be sure of in Caleb's case was that he died from what he called 'a sudden asphyxiating event of unknown causes'.

On studying Patrick's medical records he thought his ALTE was consistent with being deliberately or accidentally smothered and was of the opinion that his death too was caused by smothering.

Sarah's death was the closest to fitting a SIDS death, he said, apart from the trauma of the punctures on her face. 'As soon as there is any evidence of any trauma, that would ring alarm bells in me.'

He finally looked at the slides of Laura's heart and saw the viral myocarditis which he felt was 'most likely to have been incidental'. There was no natural explanation for any of the four children's deaths, in his opinion.

Detective Ryan knew from hundreds of hours spent on the internet that there had been examples of several children in the same family who had died from SIDS. Those cases in America had been shot down in flames. Detective Ryan knew to get to the bottom of the Folbigg case he needed to speak to those experts who had disproved the family links for SIDS and hear their views on Kathleen Folbigg and the medical histories of her children.

He wrote to the deputy commissioner of the New South Wales Police Service with what amounted to an extraordinary request from a country-town detective, let alone one who had never charged anyone with murder before. He wanted permission to fly to America and Europe to interview experts about SIDS and about mothers who murder their children. The request was passed on from the deputy commissioner to the commissioner and finally the minister before ultimately getting the green light. By this stage it was becoming clear to everyone that this was not some hick-town happening of no consequence but a major investigation into a series of murders that had the potential to make headlines not just across Australia but around the world.

As soon as he was given the all-clear, Detective Ryan wasted no time in getting his folders of material on the Folbigg murders loaded into the hold of a

Boeing 700-series jet and flying to the US midwestern city of Minneapolis to meet Dr Janice Ophoven, one of the world's leading experts on serial-killing mothers. He had already phoned her while he was putting together his brief on Kathleen Folbigg and asked her if she had heard of any similar cases before. He had come to the right person; she had worked on probably over 30 or 40 cases of children who had been killed by serial-killing mothers.

Detective Ryan had sent her material about the Folbigg case before taking microscopic slides and tissue samples to America for her to examine. When he got off the plane he was met by the local police force and shown the hospitality that is customarily extended to visiting policemen all over the world. Dr Ophoven was briefed to examine the four deaths individually and as a whole. Even at that stage Detective Ryan was aware that the legal system could find it prejudicial to view the deaths in the light of the other babies who were suffocated.

'It is one of those things that is so interesting about our world. More little children in developed countries die from trauma than any other disease and the number-one cause of trauma in babies less than a year – and the number-one killer of babies less than a year – is mums. Yet we are so horrified by the thought that when these families surface we say that we believe unbelievable things,' said Dr Ophoven.

'If you killed three women you would have the FBI all over you.'

After studying all the evidence Detective Ryan had accumulated, Dr Ophoven told him that she thought each of the children had been murdered.

In her summary she wrote:

It is my opinion, to a reasonable degree of medical certainty, that the four Folbigg children were all the victims of homicidal assaults that resulted in their suffocation. The process of suffocation will take 4 to 5 minutes to complete. During the first 1.5 to 2 minutes, while they are still fully conscious, the child will fight aggressively for their life. In small infants, this typically does not result in any external signs or physical evidence.

Important facts in this case that lead to the conclusion of homicidal suffocation include the following:

- *The autopsy fails to identify any known natural disease or disease process that could explain the sudden deaths of these infants. All four children were growing and developing normally for their age and circumstance. Despite Patrick's handicaps he was advancing well.*
- *The autopsy findings in these babies are all consistent with death by suffocation.*
- *The infants were all in the care of the same*

person at the time of their death, their mother, and she was the last person to see each of them alive.

- *None of the deaths in this case can be attributed to SIDS [Sudden Infant Death Syndrome]. It is well recognized that the SIDS process is not a hereditary problem and the statistical likelihood that 4 children could die from SIDS is in excess of 1 in a trillion.*

- *The diagnosis of SIDS requires that following a complete investigation and autopsy no other cause of death is identified. Forensic standards of practice would not allow for consideration of a second diagnosis of SIDS after a second sudden death and by the time a third child has died, the death must be investigated as a homicide.*

- *Patrick's sudden, profound and irreversible brain damage is consistent with and diagnosed as a hypoxic episode. Hypoxia in this case is synonymous with asphyxia and unfortunately heralds the fatal event in retrospect. No natural disease or process has been identified to explain this event. In my opinion, the cause of Patrick's cardio-respiratory arrest is the same process that killed him and his siblings.*

Dr Ophoven briefed Detective Ryan on the history of SIDS and the extraordinary findings in 1972 of a doctor who had effectively hijacked the entire SIDS movement and sent it down the wrong path for over 20 years. In fact, if Detective Ryan had begun his investigation just five years earlier, medical experts would have told him that it was perfectly normal for several children to die from SIDS within the one family. He would have been directed to the research conducted in 1972 by American doctor Alfred Steinschneider indicating that SIDS was linked to apnoea in babies and somehow ran in families. In other words, they would have told him that Kathleen Folbigg was the victim of a terrible series of natural catastrophes who deserved his sympathy and should not be hounded. Despite the passage of time, this was still a view he was to meet time and again from some very surprising quarters.

Dr Steinschneider had changed the way the world viewed SIDS with the publication in the October 1972 edition of the American journal *Pediatrics* of his study of five children. Two of the children M.H. and N.H. had suffered from apnoea and died despite the use of monitors. Their mother, Mrs H, explained to the doctor that she had not heard the alarm on the monitor of N.H. because she had been in the bathroom with the door closed and that M.H. had been detached from the machine just before she had died. Before the study was undertaken, Mrs H had three other children who had died in a similar way. For over

20 years this very small study was used time and again to show that SIDS was linked to apnoea and that it ran in families.

Desperate parents and doctors were given hope by Dr Steinschneider's work. At last potential SIDS victims could be identified in advance and apnoea monitors could help stop cot deaths. Sales of apnoea monitors boomed and for the next nine years Dr Stein-schneider received $5 million, almost a quarter of all the American federal government's grants, for research into SIDS.

But there was disquiet with the theory. Respected Dallas pathologist Dr Linda Norton said the paper had 'allowed homicides to continue. We don't know how many children would still be alive if it weren't for that paper'. In 1986 she was hired by the Onondaga County assistant district attorney, William Fitzpatrick, to assist with the prosecution of a man accused of smothering his daughter. While the trial was underway she said to Fitzpatrick: 'Oh, by the way. You have another homicide here in this county. You have a serial killer right here in Syracuse. It's a famous case. Take a look: *Pediatrics*, October 1972.'

Fitzpatrick later told the *Post Standard* newspaper in Syracuse:

I knew right away the kids had been murdered. If you showed me an article about five kids that died under

mysterious circumstances in the same family, I would
say to you those kids were murdered until you prove
otherwise to me. It just doesn't happen ...

Now you tell me some more things. All five of the
kids died of some sort of respiratory problem. Now,
the convincing level [that the children were murdered]
goes from 90 per cent to 95 per cent. Now, you tell me
that some of the kids had been registered at a hospital
before near-death episodes, and had been revived
heroically by the mother. Now, I'm up to 99 per cent.
Now, you tell me that all five of the kids only had
breathing difficulties when they were in the custody
and the care and the control of the mother. Now, I'm
up to 100 per cent. And all of those factors were
present in the article.

Fitzpatrick went to the Upstate Medical Centre – since
renamed the SUNY Health Science Centre – where
Dr Steinschneider had been based and went through
the old medical records to identify N.H. and M.H. He
discovered that the names of the children in the
doctor's study were Noah and Molly Hoyt, and that
their mother, Waynetta, lived in Davis Hollow in
Tioga County, 160 kilometres south of Syracuse.
Fitzpatrick did nothing more for several years until
1992 when he became district attorney. It was then
that he faxed details of the five Hoyt children's deaths
to his opposite number in Tioga County.

Police picked up Waynetta Hoyt, then aged 47, out of the blue as she was collecting her mail at the local post office. Inside the police station at Owego she admitted killing all five of her children between 1965 and 1971 because they kept crying. Now in tears herself, she said that three-month-old Eric had been smothered with a pillow; six-week-old Julie's face had been pressed into her shoulder until she stopped breathing; two-year-old James had been smothered with a bath towel; and Molly and Noah had both been smothered with pillows. She later recanted her confession but was found guilty by a jury and sentenced to 75 years of imprisonment.

Waynetta Hoyt's confession had debunked the original theory that cot deaths could run in families or were linked to apnoea. Her guilty verdict caused SIDS researchers to back-track to the early 1970s at which time all efforts had been misdirected to focus on the links between apnoea and SIDS.

An explanation for the type of actions Waynetta Hoyt had carried out was offered four months before her arrest when Canadian researchers suggested that Dr Steinschneider's original 1972 study had not chronicled the deaths of babies from SIDS but rather deaths at the hands of a mother suffering Munchausen syndrome by proxy.

Munchausen's syndrome was named in the 1950s after the wild and imaginative tall tales of the 18th-century German Baron von Munchausen. Sufferers of the syndrome invent stories of disease and illness, sometimes harming themselves, in order to get attention. Often this results in hospitalisation and surgery. In the 1970s, doctors noticed a variation on the syndrome where mothers would make up an illness in their child in order to get attention for themselves. The doctors also noticed that alleged apnoea in the child was a recurrent theme with mothers suffering from Munchausen syndrome by proxy. Mothers smothered their babies and then revived them to attract attention. British medical researchers in the 1980s found two mothers they suspected were doing this to their children. The mothers had strongly denied the allegations so the researchers went to the police and it was arranged that hidden cameras would be placed in the women's homes. Both mothers were secretly filmed placing shirts over their babies' faces to smother them. Medical professionals burst in before the mothers harmed the children and the existence of the syndrome was proved beyond doubt.

SIDS had first been defined in 1969 by Dr J. Bruce Beckwith, a paediatric pathologist in California, following pressure from parents to give a name to the mystery illness that was claiming their children's lives. He had relied on Dr Steinschneider's 1972 paper when he told investigators in Chicago that he thought the six young children of Deborah Gedzius had all died from breathing disorders. At the time Gedzius was a suspect in the shooting of her estranged husband, Delos Gedzius, who had been shot with a single bullet to the temple as he slept on the couch. The case against Gedzius for the homicide of her six children had been closed.

In the light of Waynetta Hoyt's confession in 1992, Dr Beckwith changed his mind about the deaths of the six young children in the Gedzius family. He told the media that he had made the same mistake as Dr Steinschneider and believed what the parents had said. He already thought the Hoyt children had not died from SIDS. 'I was saying these kids with familial recurrent apnoea ought to be taken out of the SIDS category, they have a different disease. But I didn't go the next step to say they might be murdered.'

Dr Beckwith still felt that up to two children in the same family could die from SIDS. But a third child? 'I'd start reaching for the handcuffs,' he was reported as saying.

One pair of hands that was certainly reaching for the handcuffs after learning of this information was that of Detective Ryan. When Dr Steinschneider's research was discredited, records of SIDS deaths in America were re-evaluated. It was found that apnoea was not linked to SIDS. It was estimated that between two and 10 per cent of SIDS cases were homicides and that nearly eight per cent of deaths of children who were being treated with apnoea monitors between 1982 and 1985 were suspected homicide victims. Despite this, the SIDS Alliance in America at the same time refused to believe the mounting evidence and insisted that less than one per cent of all SIDS babies were murdered.

Dr Ophoven told Detective Ryan: 'The reluctance to accept the concept of murderous mothers by the community at large and in particular some members of the medical community is fascinating. The political pride and turf issues that these cases bring to the surface are both intriguing and horrifying.'

This was something Detective Ryan was to find out for himself the hard way.

From America Detective Ryan flew across the Atlantic to England. Upon arrival he travelled three hours south-west from London to meet with Professor Peter Berry, a consultant pathologist at the Bristol Royal Hospital for Sick Children and Chair of Paediatric Pathologists at the University of Bristol. Professor Berry had been instrumental in getting the 'Back to Sleep' campaign started in the Northern Hemisphere in 1989, resulting in a dramatic decrease in cot deaths. The professor had come to Detective Ryan's attention for his work as co-editor of one of the largest studies of SIDS ever undertaken. The study examined the unexpected infant deaths in five healthcare regions over a period of three years. It was equivalent in size to a study of every infant death in England and Wales over a year and involved studying 450 post-mortem reports. When Detective Ryan met the professor he was told that during that entire study Professor Berry had found no 'multiple lightning bolts' striking the same family as had happened with the Folbiggs.

Detective Ryan handed over slides containing tissue samples from the four dead children, post-mortem reports, medical records and files of background details. He asked the British expert to look into the Folbigg deaths and prepare a report.

Professor Berry told the detective that it was very difficult to differentiate on the mortuary slab between a baby that had died from SIDS and one that had suffocated. In a minority of cases of suffocation there might be marks, pinpoint haemorrhages, or fresh blood coming from the nose and mouth, for example, but he stressed that such signs were only evident in a minority of cases of suffocation. He told the detective that it was often only by examining the history of the family and the circumstances of the death that those examining the body could be alert to the possibility that a particular baby might have died from suffocation, rather than SIDS.

In the case of Caleb Folbigg Professor Berry firstly dismissed the suggestion that the loose tissue around the opening of the larynx was the cause of the baby's death. 'I have searched the world literature to see if I could find any cases of death at all attributed to floppy larynx, and I came up with none . . . The natural history of floppy larynx is that it is a benign condition and just gets better with time.'

What he found far more interesting was the result of a test performed on a slide of Caleb's lung tissue that Detective Ryan had given him. 'It is believed that when some children are smothered they may bleed into their lungs and they then may recover. What happens to the blood that was in the lungs is that it is picked up by scavenger cells and turned into a substance called haemosiderin, which stains blue with this magic stain called Perl's Prussian Blue. So, a period of . . . complete occlusion of the airways leads to bleeding into the lungs. The blood is converted, over a period of 36 to 48 hours, into haemosiderin, which is recognised in the Perl's Prussian Blue stain as being blue. One of the explanations therefore, for a positive Perl's Prussian Blue stain is that there may have been an episode of previous asphyxia.'

In other words, Professor Berry found that when baby Caleb had been smothered it was not the first time it had happened. And it was not an accident. Professor Berry had stained the lung tissue of 150 infants in a study of 200 that had died suddenly. 'Within that group there were about 130, roughly,

SIDS cases. Just one of those had large amounts of haemosiderin in the air spaces in the lungs. So, it is a very unusual finding in SIDS and would lead me to exclude a case with haemosiderin from the SIDS group. I would not use the term "SIDS".'

It was understandable that this had not been picked up when the pathologist recorded Caleb's death as SIDS in 1989 – the Perl's stain test was not developed until seven years later in 1996. As this pathologist said later, he would have given a very different cause of death – the diagnosis of undetermined – and would have prompted further investigation to consider the possibility that there may have been an episode of suffocation.

In his own mind, Detective Ryan was reaching for the handcuffs again and that was only in relation to the death of the first Folbigg child. What about Patrick? Was his first acute life-threatening event and eventual death due to an epileptic seizure? Professor Berry did not think so. 'I think it is most unlikely that a first epileptic seizure coming out of the blue in an otherwise fit child would lead to this very severe brain damage. Fits are actually quite common in infants . . . febrile convulsions . . . where a baby gets a fever and has a fit. You sponge them down, cool them down, and they are fine. There have been a lot of follow-up studies to see how these children get on. They do not suffer that type of damage . . . I think it is very unlikely that a first fit would lead to such brain damage.'

Instead he thought Patrick had been suffocated. It would take only three or four minutes to suffocate a struggling child – stopping earlier could leave brain damage.

'The difference between a child being smothered and recovering and being normal, being smothered and recovering with brain damage, and being smothered and not being able to recover, must be fairly small, a matter of minutes, I would suppose,' said Professor Berry. Again, he would have recorded the cause of Patrick's death as undetermined, 'ascribing it to brain damage following an unexplained collapse'.

For Sarah's case, Professor Berry was again able to offer medical insight to the detective. Firstly he dismissed her displaced uvula as being of 'little significance'. Instead he looked at the abrasions on her face as points worth checking to see if they could have been caused during resuscitation. If they did not fit with marks made by ambulance officers in the attempts to revive her they took on a much more sinister significance.

Sarah was 10-and-a-half months old when she died. 'I think the figures are about 80 per cent of SIDS have taken place by six months of age and about three per cent or less take place after one year of age, so she is in an unusual age group for SIDS, and that would cause me to look at it a little bit more carefully.

It certainly would not exclude it from the SIDS category.'

Pathologists felt uncomfortable giving a diagnosis of 'undetermined' to the deaths of small children because it triggered an inquest which upset the families and put them through a great deal of pain. Professor Berry explained: 'What we must do is go as far as we can to protect those parents who have lost their children suddenly, tragically and naturally . . . with SIDS, from being tarred, as it were, with the same brush as those very small number of carers who may actually have harmed the child. So for me using unascertained or undetermined carefully and responsibly actually protects SIDS parents, although I do know that it puts them through a certain amount of pain at the time of the inquest. And parents have said to me, if the inquest is presented to them in the right way, actually it is a comfort for them to have gone through that process and been thoroughly investigated, and that stops the kind of tittle-tattle that goes [on] in the community when a SIDS death takes place.' Certainly this appeared to be the reason why Sarah's death was not scrutinised to a greater degree.

With respect to Laura, Professor Berry said that most pathologists would have ascribed her death to myocarditis – inflammation around the heart – when her case was viewed in isolation. He said it could also have led to an abnormal and fatal beat of the heart if she was placed under stress, such as being smothered. But Laura's death was not viewed in isolation. What it all boiled down to, as far as Professor Berry was concerned, was that in contemporary medical literature, post-Waynetta Hoyt, he was unaware of any families who had suffered three or more deaths from SIDS. 'What's more,' he told the detective, 'I'm personally not aware of any kindreds where there have been sudden deaths of previously fit children due to another medical condition that has affected three or more children . . . fatal diseases are not 100 per cent instantly fatal in every case. So, some of the genetic conditions, for example, that were excluded, have very clear presentations. They don't, in fact, present with sudden death of a previously well child.'

As Detective Ryan headed back to London's Heathrow Airport from Bristol he had a lot to think about. From what Professor Berry had told him he knew that the four Folbigg children had not died from SIDS or from a sudden disease. That left him with examining the family circumstances and the one common factor in all four deaths – the children's mother.

Detective Ryan knew that taking mothers to court for the murder of their children was a very emotive thing to do – especially in Australia. On 17 August 1980, Lindy Chamberlain had screamed into the darkened desert: 'My God, my God, the dingo's got my baby!' She was not believed and the subsequent murder trial gripped and divided the nation. Lindy Chamberlain was found guilty and imprisoned for life. Three years later she was free after new evidence saw her pardoned and her conviction quashed. Now she also lived in the Hunter Valley and her local presence was a strong reminder to the country cop of just what publicity and pitfalls lay around the corner. He had to be absolutely certain that there was a strong case against Kathleen Folbigg.

Cot death, Sudden Infant Death Syndrome, crib death – call it what you like – is as old as humankind. In the Bible, 1 Kings (3:16–27), a woman's baby is said to have 'died in the night because she overlaid it'. For centuries it was blamed on mothers rolling onto their babies while asleep. During a spate of cot deaths in America in the 1930s paediatricians blamed it on large thyroids. They would X-ray newborns and if they detected a large thymus gland they would irradiate the child to prevent cot death. The children then died from thyroid cancer.

SIDS research in the past has shown that the children of poorer people were more likely to die than wealthier people and that smoking was also linked as a contributing factor. The 'Back to Sleep' campaign got babies' noses out of the mattress, where they were suspected of re-breathing their own trapped carbon-monoxide fumes, and saved a lot of lives. But, cot deaths continue to occur. The public gets upset when mothers are accused of killing their children. SIDS remains a mystery and is hard to prove. Accusing a mother of killing four of her children was a very big call for the Singleton detective to make.

The pressure was immense. Even at the time he was in Britain, solicitor Sally Clark was tried in the glare of enormous media attention and jailed for life for murdering her two infant sons. She was later released after it was revealed that evidence had been withheld during her trial. This was something Detective Ryan did not want happening with this case. He had to get it right.

Sitting on the plane back to Australia from England, the young Singleton detective had a lot to think about. The medical experts had steered him in the direction his instincts had felt they would. His fierce determination was now backed up with strong medical evidence that showed the Folbigg children had been smothered. It was his job to prove their mother murdered them. He did not get much sleep on the long flight. By the time the jet touched down at Sydney's Kingsford-Smith Airport, Detective Ryan had a plan of action and a burning desire to see justice done.

12

Interview

NOW BACK IN AUSTRALIA, Detective Ryan took Kathy's diary to Canberra where he had it analysed at the Australian Bureau of Criminal Intelligence. Experts looked first at her handwriting and secondly used the diaries to assess her state of mind and begin to build a psychological profile. The Singleton detective swapped notes with agents from Israeli intelligence service Mossad and America's FBI. As cases of this nature had been extremely rare in Australia it was crucial for Detective Ryan to consult overseas experts, particularly the FBI who had trained psychological profilers in Australia, in order to draw on their vast resources on the subject. Detective Ryan struggled to understand the nature of the crime he was dealing with. The overseas experts, using previous cases and research that had cost millions of dollars to compile, helped him comprehend the exact nature of what he was dealing with.

Detective Ryan knew there would be no admissions in this case – Kathy and Craig had reunited – but he at least had Kathy's diary. What he read, and the analysis he received in Canberra, convinced him that this was not a case he wanted to relinquish or put on the back-burner. Rather than sitting back, Detective Ryan increased the stakes. He successfully mounted a strong and convincing case to the Supreme Court for listening devices to be fitted in the Folbiggs' house. There was no need to enter the house to tap the phone; that was done through the telephone exchange. But to hear what was being said in the house meant a police technician had to physically enter the house and place the bugs. Detective Ryan coordinated the operation. Undercover police officers placed the house under static surveillance and took note of Kathy and Craig's routine. Once that had been assessed, undercover officers tailed each of them as they left the house. They remained in constant radio contact with the officers at the house to warn them if either of the Folbiggs made a sudden and unexpected return home. The police technician surreptitiously broke into the house and placed the bugs without being caught. Tapes were made of every conversation that occurred in the house in July and August 1999.

Once the bugs had been fitted Detective Ryan began to rattle the Folbiggs' cage to get them talking. On 23 July 1999 Kathleen Folbigg came to the front door to find two policemen standing on the doorstep.

'Mrs Folbigg, I'm Detective Ryan. This is Detective Engdahl. Do you remember me?'

'Yes,' said Kathy.

'Mrs Folbigg, the investigation has come to a state where I now wish to interview you in relation to the death of all the children. Are you prepared to come to the police station to be interviewed?' asked Detective Ryan.

'Yes. Can I have a shower first?'

'Of course. Take your time,' said the policeman, who was invited to wait in the dining room with his colleague while Kathy showered and changed.

She emerged a little while later. 'Will I come with you or can I drive down myself?' she asked.

'It's up to you,' said Detective Ryan.

Kathy elected to drive herself there and followed the police officers back to the station. As he looked in his rear-view mirror, Detective Ryan saw that Kathy was talking on her mobile phone. They took the New England Highway past Teasdales motor dealership where Craig worked. He was standing outside on the footpath talking into his mobile phone as they drove past. Craig then jumped into his own car and joined the procession down to the police station. Detective Ryan intercepted him at the station and told him he could not sit in on his wife's interview. Kathy reassured Craig she would be okay, that she did not want anybody with her, and went into the stark, cream-coloured interview room with the two policemen while Craig returned to work.

It was a long and gruelling session that lasted over eight hours and was recorded on 27 audiotapes and nine videotapes. Detective Ryan sat at the interview table within easy reach of the audio- and videotape machines that recorded the entire procedure. Opposite him sat Detective Senior Constable Marita Engdahl. At the end of the table sat Kathy. It was 9.26am when the tapes started rolling.

'We are making inquiries into the deaths of Caleb, Patrick, Sarah and Laura Folbigg. Do you understand that?' asked Detective Ryan.

'Yep,' said Kathy.

The police ran through the preliminaries with Kathy. She stated her date of birth – 14 June 1967 – and confirmed her address and her understanding that she was free to leave at any time. They then went into the birth, life and death of Caleb, Patrick and Sarah. She drew diagrams of each of the homes where her children had died.

Kathy appeared to be holding things together very well. A police interview is not like a cross-examination in court where hard questions can be pressed home. It merely elicits information that the interviewee is prepared to give in response to police questioning. The interview does not cast doubt on or attack implausible answers. It is a skill to conduct a good police interview. And Detective Ryan was to prove very skilful indeed.

When questioned about Laura, Kathy described how she took her home the day she died and 'plonked' her on the bed.

'And what did you do after you put her in the bed?' asked Detective Ryan.

'Went back out and then I usually, if I didn't get to wash up or do any of that sort of thing, then I used to do it while she was asleep. We used to have – we have still got it, I think – a listening monitor that used to be on all the time in her room and I used to carry the other bit around with me. So, hangin' out washin' and all that sort of thing I could still hear what she was doing. Especially 'cause we started shutting doors we had it on all the time. So I just would have been house cleaning. I normally did the house cleaning if I got a chance while she was asleep. Just picking up the toys, never anything noisy like the major vacuuming or anything like that, but, yeah, I always did all the rest . . . The morning that she died I'd actually gone outside to check on the dogs because we have got one dog that likes to chuck a Houdini and escape all the time, and I'd actually gone out to check on her so I was right out the back. I don't think I had the monitor piece with me because . . . I think I left it in the kitchen because sometimes havin' it on you . . . annoys you so you put it on the bench or whatever. So, I was out the back checking on the dog. She wasn't there so it took me a little while to figure out whether she was in the yard or whether she had done a Houdini and was gunna have to go out the front to try and find her. Then she sort of appeared so that was okay. Then I've gone back inside, walked up the hallway, thought I'll check on her . . . as I've done a thousand times before; I'll check on her, I've been gone long enough, I'll see if she's still all right. And that's when, yeah, when I've sort of walked in the room and noticed she was on her back. So I thought all right, that's it, I'm sort of rollin' you over girl . . . and it all just went from there, the scoopin' her out of bed and the CPR and all the rest of it.'

If the interview had been a cross-examination in court Detective Ryan would have picked up the inconsistency between this account of events and the version Kathy had told him on the day Laura died. Back then she had told Detective Ryan she had gone inside to check on Laura because she had heard her coughing. Now she completely forgot she had said this.

In the police interview, Kathy sailed on with her version of events. Detective Ryan listened very intent-ly, preparing to fire back questions at Kathy as the morning wore on.

After lunch, he said: 'Now Craig tells us that after Caleb died you appeared to get over it easier than he did. What can you tell me about that?'

'I don't know,' said Kathy. 'That's just the persona of me, I suppose . . . [I]t's been explained to me now after going to counselling and therapy sessions that I . . . tend to maybe not deal with it, but I tend to put it away or lock it somewhere and choose just to move on and try to go forward rather than hanging around back in the past or – or that sort of thing. Something of which I'm now trying to get out of the habit of doing because it serves no purpose to do that . . . If I appeared to be handling it better it was probably more of a case of I just blocked and locked rather than actually deal with the situation at the time. I still have a tendency to do that. I'm probably at some level doing it to a point now where I'm not quite as bad as I used to be. That's something we've both figured out.'

The detective was picking up fresh inconsistencies from the morning session of questioning with Kathy compared to Craig's earlier statements. Someone had to be lying. 'Craig tells me that he picked up Caleb and you were standing there with your hands to your head and that you didn't pick up Caleb. What can you tell me about that?'

'He could be right,' said Kathy, back-pedalling. 'I thought I'd picked him up. When you asked me today I thought I'd picked him up, but you know . . . Present it to me like that, that could be the case. If I was screaming and not saying his name like I thought I was, there's a great chance I was standing there with my hands on my head and just – so yeah. I don't specifically remember; it's too accurate.'

Detective Ryan then began to question Kathy on her diary entries around the time of Caleb's death. Firstly he produced her black A4 Superior diary from 1989 and pointed out the entry for 19 February at 2am, which read: '*Finally asleep!!!*'

'Can you tell me why you wrote that?' asked Detective Ryan.

'Because he might have been a bit restless, and he was asleep. We might have had a bit of trouble. Yeah, I reckon, yeah, that's all.

'I used to write in diaries as . . . basically they were sort of like a vent or a release. I used to sort of write things that I was doin' that day, or anything that might have bothered me in the slightest I used to write in a diary rather than talk to [Craig], which I've learnt now not to do. And it could be something totally stupid as I've forgotten to go and pay a bill down the street or go and get the milk, or at the end if I had a spare minute it'll be just whatever popped into my head at the time and I'd write it down . . . I don't do it any more . . .'

'You said that you learn now not to do so,' said Detective Ryan.

'Mm hmm.'

'What do you mean by that?'

'Because we had an altercation once where he'd actually – I dunno if it was that diary or not – but he'd actually read one and I struck that as invading my space and that's a personal thing that he shouldn't have done. I wouldn't say that there was anything in it that should have upset him too much . . . I used to call them babble books 'cause that's exactly what I used to do in them sort of thing. And, but just the mere fact that he'd sort of not asked me first. If he had come and said to me "Can I read this?", I probably would have said "Yeah". But it was sort of, I sprung him reading it; well that's a different kettle of fish. Or find out after the fact that he's read it . . . So it was probably only, to be truthful, Mother's Day this year I decided not to write in them any more, so yeah. 'Cause I had written in a few and on Mother's Day this year I sort of pulled one out to have a look and I've flicked back at what I'd written and pretty much decided that life's pretty crappy and I shouldn't be writin' it down and reminding myself of all these things, and I just got rid of them all . . . and I haven't written in one since.'

The diary Craig had found covered the period of Patrick's life and one particular entry, written after Patrick had been diagnosed as blind, particularly intrigued the detective. 'There's an entry in there about you considering leaving both Patrick and Craig,' Detective Ryan began.

'Yeah, I was sort of sufferin' a bit,' said Kathy. 'You've sort of got to understand it. As I said, 99 per cent of my time was for Patrick . . . there was no time for myself . . . and unfortunately when traumatic things happen to me I tend to want to do what's known as a runner; I tend to want to sort of run from the actual situation. I started thinking to myself maybe it'll be good if I just left Patrick with Craig and he might be cared for just as well or whatever. I started to think the two of them could survive quite easily without me. And that all comes from spendin' so much time lookin' after Patrick and not bein' able to spend any time lookin' after Craig or myself. I just started to think I wanted to do the runner bit, the flight bit. I s'pose it's the flight-or-fight syndrome that you invariably hear of all over the place, and I was gettin' to the flight stage. But I sort of worked through that and thought, okay, no I can't do that, I've gotta stay and look after him. And I truly didn't think that Craig would actually cope lookin' after Patrick on his own. He's, yeah, he's the sort of person that requires a bit of support and help when you're doin' anything major or anything like that, so I changed my mind and decided not to.'

Detective Ryan moved on to the night Sarah died and asked Kathy if there had been a battle of wills that night.

'Probably,' said Kathy. 'Used to be a regular thing I s'pose. Craig used to comment about it so it must have been happening regularly, yeah. It wasn't so much a battle of the wills to the point where I would become frustrated or, yes I would become frustrated but never angry at her because she would not go to sleep. I would always end up reasoning to myself as I was walkin' up the hallway to go to bed myself that she's a baby and it's illogical to her. If she's just awake and wants to play, why should she be going to bed? So that's what I used to end up thinking as I was walking up the hallway . . . It would start out as a battle of the wills I s'pose; I'd get a bit stressed and frustrated and then think: "All right, fair enough, you can have it your own way." As long as she sleeps somewhere . . . So by that stage Craig had sort of figured out when; he managed to pick up the signs and he would just say: "Look, I'll take her." And that's when I started to go off to bed myself and just leave it to them to do what they wanted. So yeah.'

'What signs?'

'He reckoned I'd get a bit snappy and like stomping around the house sort of thing, but that'd be about it. I don't recall anything else.'

'Craig says that he heard you make an angry growling noise that night.'

'Probably. Sometimes I'll do that now, but I dunno if it's a growl or what it is, but yeah, if something's frustrating me I'll express myself and be done with it. But it's never something that hangs on; I'm not that sort of person.'

By now Detective Ryan was getting to the heart of the matter. With each of the children he returned to inconsistencies between Craig's version of what had happened, Kathy's earlier version, and what she had now just told him. 'You told us before that Sarah actually went to bed for some time and then awoke and started playing with Craig. That's what you told me before.'

'Right,' said Kathy.

'And now you're telling me that on this night she didn't go to sleep and she was just given to Craig. Now, what can you tell me about that inconsistency?'

'I don't know,' said Kathy. 'I recall, as I said, I recall her going to bed. I don't sort of recall having too much trouble with her until you read what Craig's written, but yeah, I can't explain the inconsistency . . . With my kids I choose to remember all the good bits; I don't choose to remember the difficulty or the hard bits . . . The hard bits with Patrick was part of his life, as in his epilepsy and caring and his blindness and all that sort of thing. But with sitting here now and trying to recall whether or not they gave me a hard time the night before and all that sort of thing, it's probably a case of I choose not to remember that; I choose to remember that, you know, they were pretty good kids and so on.'

Now the detective produced the diary that Craig had brought to the police station. 'Can you tell me the conversation that you had with Craig about him bringing this diary to the police station?' asked Detective Ryan.

'I wasn't happy . . . but he said that there was a few passages in it that he didn't understand himself, so he asked me some questions about it and I answered them. He hasn't brought it up again since . . .'

Detective Ryan asked Kathy to read out the entry for 18 June 1996. Even she had trouble deciphering it. '*Baby plans are still on the go.* God, that's terrible writing. *Could be preggy,* I think that says now. *Won't find out until next month. That could create a problem if my body's not in peak condition, it may not accept pregnancy . . . I'm ready this time and I'll have help and support this time. When I think I'm going to lose control like the last times, I'll just hand baby over to someone else and not feel so totally alone. Getting back into my exercise after will help my state of mind, and sleeping whenever possible as well. I have learnt my lesson this time.*'

'What do you mean by "*Lose control like the last times*"?' asked Detective Ryan.

'The frustration that I felt with Sarah every now and then, the frustration that I felt with Patrick. They were never frustrations that were detrimental to the kids in any way; it was usually always directed at myself or at Craig. And I meant keeping in control as in not keeping control as such, but sort of keeping control and learning to voice an objection or voice if I've got a problem. Instead of trying to handle everything myself, let other people sort of do it for me.'

'And what about, "*I've learnt my lesson this time*"?'

'As in the frustration area I was probably thinking of more there. Not to let the frustration get the better of me and learning to actually talk and communicate more,' replied Kathy.

The detective then asked Kathy to read out the entry for 21 July 1996. Again she stumbled as she tried to read it. '*I truly deserve everything life throws at me . . . the philosophy is whatever happens, happens, and it's the way it should be. I'm going to try my hardest this time. If anything does happen I'll just leave and try and let Craig go in peace and start again. No I wouldn't, I'm not that brave. Really, I depend on people and other people's help too much.* It doesn't make any sense, but yeah.'

Detective Ryan asked: 'What do you mean by, "*If anything does happen*"?'

'I was referring to if fate was cruel and it happened again, which it was, yeah.'

'Why should you have to try your hardest this time?'

'Because I felt the last few times . . . that I obviously hadn't tried hard enough. There was something that I could have done or hadn't done or should have done, so that statement was that I felt that I needed just to try to pay more attention and not miss anything, that's all.'

Kathy was then asked to read out the entry for

26 August 1996 in which she wrote about going to a clairvoyant.

'Do you believe in that?' asked Detective Ryan.

'Not really. The ones I went to sort of said things and you've gone: "That's a bit eerie." But I don't think I'm sort of, you know? I've actually got an aunty on my real side of the family that thinks she might be one, so I get a bit more exposed to it than I probably should now, but I don't sort of really have an opinion about it one way or the other.'

'Do you think the children are somewhere else now?'

'I'd like to think they are. You always like to think if you've lost your child that it hasn't gone somewhere horrible. You'd like to think that they're somewhere where they're happy.'

'What do you mean by "*Even though I am responsible it's all right*"?'

'I was still carrying around the thought that I could have done more or should have done more. So the word "responsible" in there sort of refers to that: my thoughts of I didn't try enough or didn't do something, I should have done something. So to me that's what my word "responsible" means.'

'When you say "*She accepts it and is happy there*", who's she?'

'I think I was referring to Sarah. The clairvoyant, I asked the clairvoyant sort of about it. The eerie bit was that she saw four children and I said: "No I haven't got four children." She said: "But you had three" or something along those lines, and I think she said, "Was there anything that you wanted me to ask, you wanted to ask me?" I think I must have just asked, "Is she happy?" or something, and she said, "Yes." So that's referring to the clairvoyant.'

Kathy was then asked about the diary entry for 30 October 1996 where she worried that her next child would '*suffer my psychological mood swings like the others did*'.

'I didn't mean suffer as in a physical suffering of any kind; I meant it more as, you know, your child picks up when you're upset about something or not happy about something . . . they'll pick up on that,' explained Kathy.

'This second sentence,' asked Detective Ryan. ' "*I pray I'm prepared and ready, mind wise for the next one.*" Is that saying that you weren't sure if you were ready?'

'Always doubts. I'm never havin' another child as long as I live, but even if the possibility was there you'd always doubt whether you were actually ready for it, especially after, you know? So Craig and I have gone into having Laura and have not doubted whether or not we were ready for it; just would have been . . . totally unheard of.'

At this point Detective Senior Constable Engdahl came in with a question. 'You just said a minute ago that you're never having another child as long as you live. Is that how you feel now or was that your thoughts at the time?'

'No, no, no, that's, yeah. I've always sort of gone, with these four I've always gone through a period, especially always straight after. It's always been, "No, no, that's it, we're not doin' it again". With this particular one with Laura there's just, if I could book myself into the hospital and go and have a tubular ligation or one of those operations I would, and Craig's already suggested that he would quite happily go in and book and get himself a vasectomy so that we never face or go through this again. So the only reason that I don't go is that the last time I had thought of never having children, that was straight after Sarah. It's a natural emotion that you sort of think "No, I'm never doing that again". I actually inquired about having an operation and doing all that sort of thing and was told that the doctors won't even touch me for 12 months because it's a –'

'So you're saying that you'll give yourself another bit of time to really make sure that you don't change your mind. Is that right?'

'That's right, yeah. I don't intend to change my mind but it's, yeah. I'm just waiting for the time period to lapse before I walk into a doctor and say, okay, this is the situation now, we'll do something about it, sort of thing.'

For her diary entry of 4 December 1996 Kathy was prompted to explain why she thought Craig had been looking at her with an expression of blame. 'I didn't ever want Craig to look at me like he has done with Laura and all of this, and turn around and say, you know, ask me what's happened but have that certain look in his eye where you've sort of really gotta try and explain yourself right down to a detail or otherwise he'll over-analyse it and look at you a different way. It sort of, I just didn't wanna have to ever go through that again, which I have, and sort of gone through that, and Craig and I have tried to, you know, with the help of [our therapist] and therapy again we've tried to work past all that.'

'Did you ask for help with sleep whenever you could?' asked Detective Ryan.

'Yeah, yeah I did. See, Laura was sort of different. I recall her as being a brilliant sleeper, so I don't think I ever sort of had a regular where I was sort of, I won't lie, by the time Laura come around, as it's evident here writin' at four, half past four in the bloody mornin' and half past three and whatever else, I didn't sleep too well as it was. But by then it was a pattern I'm used to. I'm now used to only sleeping two, three hours myself, so . . . I don't regard it as a big deal. But back when, you know, Caleb and Patrick were around, especially Caleb, you're looking at someone who used to sleep 12 hours straight, so it's a big sort of thing.'

Detective Ryan picked up on a phrase in the diary entry for 1 January 1997: '*stress made me do terrible things*' and asked Kathy what she meant by her words.

'As in have an angry thought here or there. I don't think I've met a parent that doesn't have an angry thought every now and again if their child's arguin' with them or somethin's not goin' quite right or it's just not happening . . . well, take Sarah for example; when she wouldn't go to sleep, sure, the battle of wills would kick in, the frustration would kick in and, yes, I would have an angry thought, but it was never to harm her: it was always why wasn't Craig here to help me, you know?'

Kathy went on to explain why having stresses and angry thoughts were a terrible thing. 'You hear of some parents and situations where that angry thought or frustration just develops into something that's nasty, and to me that's – you know? It never happened with me but in retrospect I sit here now and look back on my children and think obviously my frustrations and the odd angry thought exasperated my situations and made them worse than what they probably could have been if I'd have mellowed out and just let them pretty much do what they wanted to do.'

The diary entry of 4 February 1997 described Kathy's guilt for how responsible she felt for her children. She told Detective Ryan what she meant by this unclear statement. 'Did I try enough, did I do enough, was I where I was supposed to be, was I not trying hard enough, was I, all the things that I thought responsibility was.'

'Do you seriously think that you are responsible for your children's deaths?' he asked.

'I regarded it, and I still sometimes do now, which I'm tryin' to work through with Fitchett [the therapist], that it was a failure of mine somewhere along the lines if I couldn't keep my children alive and with me.'

'How have you failed?'

'Didn't do something, didn't walk in the room two minutes earlier, didn't check two seconds earlier, I didn't do something that would have meant when I walked in the room that they were alive and well instead of when I walked in the room they weren't sort of thing.'

Referring to the diary entry again, Detective Ryan asked, 'Why do you say you were a terrible mother?'

'Because they weren't there with me, no other reason. I look at other mothers who can be poppin' out five, six, seven, eight of them, probably havin' even more stress and trouble than I have ever had in my lifetime with that many of them but they were all still there. The parents who are nasty to their kids in public and you look at them and think, well, good grief, you poor kid. They're still there. And to me . . . at that time in my life I was wondering whether I was a strong enough and good enough mother to make sure this one stayed with me. And now I sit here and –'

'That doesn't make you a terrible mother,' said Detective Senior Constable Engdahl.

Kathy began to cry. 'It's a perception that I've got to get over, that's all.'

'Why were you scared of being alone with the baby?' asked Detective Ryan.

'Because I had pretty much decided that since these terrible things kept happening when I was by myself I didn't want to be by myself. It was a way of self-protecting myself I suppose. Stupid because this doesn't happen; you have got to spend time with your child. It's probably why with Laura I went back to the gym early and got straight out of the house. We barely even – unless she was havin' a nap – spent time at home by ourselves. We were always out and about, call in to see Craig, go around to somebody's house . . . It was just another way to try and avoid what happened but it didn't work.'

The gruelling eight-hour interview finally concluded at exactly 5.48pm with Kathy even more tearful. But her troubles had only really just begun.

13
Tap Tap

AT THE CONCLUSION of the interview Detective Ryan told Kathy that he was going to search both her flat in Andrew Street and the house in Millard Close. He had search warrants for both places. 'We are looking for other diaries which relate to the death of your children. Do you have any more diaries?'

'I've just started a new diary and it's up at the house,' said Kathy.

Kathy – tense, tired and spent – and a posse of four policemen went to the flat first. They took a few miscellaneous items from the flat and then went on to the house. Once again Detective Ryan asked if there were any more diaries that she had forgotten about. Kathy replied that she had bought one yesterday and went to the main bedroom and collected the new 1999 personal diary from the built-in wardrobe. The police officers then began to search the house. After a few minutes one of them, Sergeant Gralton, found another diary in the wardrobe of the main bedroom.

'I didn't know it was there. I thought it was gone,'

said Kathy, who had mentioned during the interview that she thought she had thrown all her diaries away on Mother's Day that year.

The four officers collected a few other papers relating to the children, including their blue medical booklets that contained records of their immunisations, physical and mental progress, and medical check-ups, and left Kathy to ponder her fate. Craig had been waiting anxiously at home for her since she had phoned him that morning on the way to the police station. They had a lot to talk about. Unknown to them, the police tapes were running.

Craig was trapped. He knew that on the night of Sarah's death the light had been on and Kathy had been up with Sarah just minutes before the toddler died. Craig was sticking his head in the sand to save his marriage. He had changed his statement with the police and felt he would look mean and vindictive if he tried to change it back. Besides, now he was back with Kathy and he was working hard to keep peace and harmony at home. After all, she had been a good mother 99 per cent of the time. The kids were always clean and well cared for. They had never been physically abused. She had always kept the house tidy for her family. What more could a man ask for, really? Right then, in July, he was trying to forget the other one per cent of Kathy's behaviour as a mother. He loved her. They had shared 15 years together, good times and bad. True, Kathy's anger was a frightening force but the upside of that passion was her warmth and personality, which kept drawing him back to her.

Kathy had a few questions of her own for Craig. She was tight-lipped with anger. 'Bernie said something about the night Sarah died,' she began. Kathy recalled that she had put Sarah to bed. But then Detective Ryan had pointed out the difference between Craig's and Kathy's story. She told Craig she had 'totally forgotten' about him confronting her because Sarah would not go to sleep. 'You said that I had walked into the lounge room and threw her at you. My first response was that I never threw my children anywhere, thank you very much. And then I basically had to say, I don't remember a conversation and I don't remember doing that.' Detective Ryan had caught them in a lie and Kathy was not happy.

Craig was on the back foot and tap dancing by this stage. Stuttering and faltering he desperately attempted to explain himself. 'Yeah, I, I mean, I can remember the night she wouldn't go to sleep, so I walked up the hallway and then I just told . . . I mean, that they are interpreting the words "throw" from what I said. I, I was sitting on the lounge and you were about a foot away from the edge of the lounge and just went to – and, uh, then you went to bed and then I sat up and then you came in.'

They were both very emotional. It was self-

206

preservation for him but he was also desperate not to ruin the relationship. Kathy, meanwhile, wanted to know why he had gone to the police in the first place.

By now Craig was stuttering and faltering even more. 'I went there because I was so full of hate and spite and anxiety and grief and anguish over the fact that I'd not only lost my daughter, I'd lost my wife. You know, I'd lost the two most precious things to me – not possessions, but people who . . . a person who I had built my whole existence on.

'I'm sorry to say that – that's the truth. I couldn't see that I would function with anybody else . . . I stood in church in front of a man of God and swore my whole life to you until I die because I loved you and I've never . . . it's wavered yeah . . . it's changed you know . . . but it's never failed, never disappeared.

'I wanted to stay with you because we've both been through the same things. We'd both shared these losses, so therefore we should share life with these losses.

'I wanted to stay with you because years and years ago when I met you, I never wanted to not be with you. It didn't appear to me . . . I didn't know how to voice that in what I felt was a romantic way that would sway you or anything like that. I was so frustrated; I was hurting, so I thought: fine, I'll fucking fix this.

'I'll fuck your life, you fucked mine, I'll fuck yours. I'll go and tell some horrible things about you that the police think you did anyway. And I couldn't do it.

Went there to do it, started to do it, couldn't do it . . . but when I told . . . that that was the case, he said, well, you know . . .' he trailed off lamely.

Craig's attempt at an explanation fell short of completely placating Kathy but it had defused the situation somewhat. She had now relaxed a little and trusted him enough to recount the police interview to him. She asked if he thought it sounded as if she had shown enough emotion in the right places. 'Did I cry in the right spot? You know, was I sounding pathetic enough for them, you know just stupid friggin' shit like that?'

They continued to talk late into the night and finally went to bed. They had papered over some of the cracks in their marriage but the distrust brought about by Craig's first visit to the police station was lying dangerously close to the surface. In bed, long after Craig had fallen into his usual deep sleep, Kathy tossed and turned. Her mind raced with scenarios and possibilities.

Over the next few days Kathy role-played answering questions she anticipated she might be asked by the authorities in the coming weeks about the deaths of her children – questions that were her worst nightmares. She acted out questions and answers in what she thought was the privacy of her own home.

The day after her interview she was heard on tape

talking to herself in an American accent as though rehearsing an interview between a lawyer and witness in her case. Recreating the courtroom scene in the house she first took the role of lawyer and asked herself: 'Considering that you actually know her . . . do you think that you are capable of an unbiased report considering . . . circumstantial at the best. Attempting to accuse my client of murdering all four of her children. What are your thoughts on that?'

'Um, I don't have thoughts on that. I don't have thoughts on that,' she replied to herself.

Back in lawyer mode she asked herself: 'Does she strike you as a sort of person that would, considering that you know her slightly?'

'No, she doesn't but it's not to say that I won't see the other side and change my mind. It's not to say that I wouldn't see the other side and change my mind,' she answered.

As Kathy prepared to face the difficult times ahead, the police tapes continued to roll.

Three days after the interview, the rows, the pressure, and the uncertainty were continuing in the Folbigg household. The cage had been well and truly rattled and the police tapes were recording every second of the fallout between Kathy and Craig. Early in the morning, in the middle of another heated discussion,

Craig even suggested, in an attempt to reassure Kathy how preposterous the police case was against her, that he could just as easily also be suspected by Detective Ryan of having killed the children. 'Hold on a minute, hold on a minute, hold on a minute; can you hear me out? All right, so I get up and I kill Caleb because the next person to find him would be you, all right? Sarah: you're out of the room, I wake up, I admit that I wake up at 1 o'clock, I kill her in her sleep while you're out of the room . . . It's not ridiculous. It's as feasible as what they're trying to say about you . . . All I'm trying to show to you is the futility of the bullshit he's going on.'

Later, Craig would explain in court that he said many of the things that were caught on tape because he did not want to argue with his wife. To avoid arguments he either told her what he thought she wanted to hear or he escaped to the garage to get out of her way.

But that night, after their heated discussion hours ago in the early morning, Craig told Kathy that he was sick of her talking about it and was determined not to let the police persecute her. In the privacy of their own home Craig was passionate in his defence of his wife against Detective Bernie Ryan. 'I don't want him going after you for something you didn't do. That, you and I know. I knew you didn't do it like you know I didn't do it . . . maybe what we're doing now is what he wants us to do, sit there and have factional fights instead of joint, cohesive support.

'I really wanted to pose all that to you to show you're not a wicked person either, but I can be a wicked person, I can be the deviate person, how I sell motor cars. I use whatever I can to my advantage to sell a motor car, whether it's my children's lives or my children's deaths. When Laura was alive, I used the fact that she was alive and part of my life as an advantage to sell a motor car.'

He repeated the same lines to Kathy's family. At that stage, her foster sister, Lea Bown, was convinced that the police were conducting a witch-hunt. When Lea's daughter, Tanya, rang the Folbiggs on 26 July concerned about Kathy's police interview, Craig told her that Detective Ryan 'planted some bullshit in my head when I was at me lowest point there when Kath had left me.

'He's just trying to assassinate her character,' Craig continued.

He then tried to reassure Tanya that she would not be quizzed by the detective. 'He's obviously not going to talk to people who are in favour of Kathy.'

'I mean he hasn't been really . . . following people up who we originally spoke to who had good things to say about her and how she was as a mother, you know. He's not going to go and build a case that's good for her.'

The Folbiggs and everyone close to them were very

emotional at the time. It was only months since Laura had died and Craig was back in complete denial about his wife. Once again he believed in her. Craig's earlier suspicions that he had taken to Detective Ryan may have been gnawing at the back of his mind but he had pushed them far from his consciousness. His family was also looking for explanations for his two very different trips to the police station in May.

On the same day that Tanya called, Craig also spoke on the phone to his sister Carol Newitt. The conversation was similar to the one he had had with Tanya. Craig told his sister that Detective Ryan had made it clear he would be asking her questions about the time they lived near each other in Newcastle when Patrick had been alive. 'He's trying to assassinate Kath's character. That's all he's doing . . . What he's trying to do is trying to establish that she couldn't cope as a mother.'

'No, well, I wouldn't say that. I wouldn't say that,' said his sister. She went on to give an example of what she saw as Kathy's good parenting, how she had only ever seen Kathy's concern and good care of the children.

'But, but, he'll – I mean – if you say – if you say what you just said to me, he'll, he'll take it that she was scared of what she was going to do to the kid,' said Craig.

'Oh.'

'That's why he's bending things, you see?' said

Craig. At that time he thought the detective was too gung ho and was trying to become famous. He told his sister they could 'fix his wagon' by either going on the television show 'Sally Jesse Raphael' or otherwise by not saying anything to the policeman at all.

'You know what I mean. I listened to the tapes of them grilling Kath down at the station, you know, and they asked her to explain something that she'd written in her diary from years ago and . . . you could tell he wasn't happy . . . with the answer. So he'd try and twist it all you know? He did that with me. He planted horrible things in my head and brought me to . . . from going in there and originally being horrible, but then recanting it all, you know? I mean, he started that. Come and saw me at the car yard,' said Craig.

'Yeah, well,' said Carol.

'He said to me: "Suppose you feel pretty bad, you know. I mean, she's cleaned out, and she's going out with her girlfriends and going to the gym and you're all alone . . . haven't got your kid and your wife's walked out on you and, you know, isn't it all pretty convenient for her?" – and all that sort of shit.'

On the same night, Craig also talked to a female friend on the phone where he discussed the way the police were pursuing them. 'They're on this bent, mate. They're just on this bent and they're, you know, they're failing – as I said to Kaz [his sister Carol] – they're failing to see that we're victims as well as the kids. Yeah, it's just horrible, mate. It's horrible. Like Kaz, you know, Kaz got a bit upset there tonight on the phone and she said, "I don't know how yous are coping because it's like they're not giving you any ability to sit back and say, 'fuck me, we've lost our baby'." You know. Like, like, we've lost Laura and, and I said to Kaz: "It's like they're taking the right off us to grieve." '

The police tapes recorded Craig's female telephone caller agreeing with him. 'I said that to Carol earlier on tonight. They've taken away your grieving time.'

'Well . . . they're convinced Kathy has no remorse or sorrow for Laura not being with us, but they don't see what she's like here.'

'Yeah, but you know.'

'You know, they don't see what she's like in private, which is that she's an intensely private person,' said Craig.

'Because they don't know Kathy.'

Craig murmured his agreement.

His friend continued. 'They don't know how she operates . . . I think . . . they're sort of trying to draw up a profile. Well, to me Kathy is a strong, intensely private feeling person.'

'She holds my hand when we go out, but she doesn't hang off me . . . I mean she's intensely private of her emotions and affections for me. You know . . . the affection she shows me behind closed doors here, she doesn't show me outside. She'll hold my hand; she'll give me a kiss hello and goodbye. Like, it's not even a pasho, you know?' said Craig. Continuing his complaints about Detective Ryan, he added: 'What also narks him too is anybody sitting there waxing lyrical about how good a mother she was when they saw her as a mother. You know what I mean? . . . He don't want to hear that . . . He's been up here like on Saturday trying to drive a wedge between us and that didn't work. Oh you know, I mean, he already tried that with me on my own down the car yard and . . . he nearly got it to work. But . . . I was lucky – I got to my senses, well, a bit too late, but soon enough, you know. Silly thing I did, but you'll hear about that. But then he's here on Saturday trying to drive a wedge between us and I think he sees that divided we fall and united we stand, and that narks him, because he said to Kath on Friday night, you know, "I suppose you're going to leave him again" and then they followed us on Saturday night, tailed us and followed us, and they're just trying to rattle our cage, you know, and like I said to Kath, he's trying to unhinge us and see whether we turn into frightened rabbits, you know, because frightened rabbits run and hide, don't they?'

Later Craig would admit that he did, in fact, feel like a frightened rabbit. But on the phone that day he had plenty more to say.

'As Kath said, he's just doing his job like a bulldog

would . . . he's on a mission, you know. Think he's got hold of something and it's going to make him famous.'

'Well, it would make him famous if it was true,' said the caller.

'Yeah, I suppose,' laughed Craig.

'God, we've got like a fucking multi-murderer on our hands, if it's true.'

Craig laughed again.

'Christ, you know, he's going to be in every paper in the fucking world. And you know, *Woman's Day* will be knocking on his door for the story.'

'Yeah, but I'm going to hire Harry M. Miller,' said Craig.

'Yeah, beat him at his own game.'

'It's a bit of a joke, isn't it?'

'Well, suppose you've got to find humour in situations otherwise you go mental, don't you?' said the female caller.

'Yeah, I mean . . . he's looking down his nose at Kath especially, but the both of us. Like, because she goes to the gym, she works part-time, we go out and dance and drink and socialise with people and all that, and that's like, you know, what are you supposed to do, crawl up and die? Life's fucking got to go on and you know what I mean; they don't see how hard it is to go on with that.'

Even as he said this Craig was wondering why, in

his relationship with Kathy, that, even if life had to go on, it had to go on as if Laura had never existed. He still wondered why, as far as his wife was concerned, the past had never happened.

However, during his phone conversation with his friend, he explained his philosophy of going out. Kathy was going out, with or without him, and with no Laura at home he chose not to stay at home alone with his memories. 'What do you do? Sit in the house and fester, and you know, it is hard being in the house for both of us. You know, she's not here, fuck this, let's go out.'

He also revealed to his friend the key to his managing to keep going despite losing four children and what he told people who reckoned they would not be able to continue living if they lost a child. 'I said to [Detective Ryan] on Saturday, you know, what amazes me, people come up and go: "I see that little fellow there of mine. If I lost him, I couldn't cope. I think I'd fucking kill myself." I say to them: "Bullshit. Bull fucking shit, mate. You wake up every day. It's another fucking day." '

Later Craig would explain this time he shared with Kathy while their conversations were under surveillance and also justify the extraordinary conversations he had with his family. 'People were wondering how we were both going with the situation, that the police had made it evident that they were investigating Kathy into the events of the children's deaths. So people were wondering how we were going. I had already been and told all the lies I had told for the reason I had told them, so I was pretty much trapped by that time, so I just kept on telling people what they needed to hear, because I didn't want to tell my family that I had been to the police and lied.'

As the tapes rolled for the next few weeks Craig would discover he was not the only one who was lying. He later recalled coming home and finding Kathy sitting in the bath crying, her arms wrapped around her knees. His heart had gone out to her. To comfort her, he had made her a cup of tea and gone in to sit with her. Their conversation upset him and made him feel guilty for the part he had played in incriminating her. She made it clear to him that she was crying because she no longer had Laura and the police were investigating her. Yet months later, as the police net closed in on Kathy and the marriage disintegrated, she walked up to him and said: 'I was crying because I'm trapped here, 'cause I don't want to be here and I'm trapped here.'

All that Craig had done to protect his wife had been for nothing. Kathleen Folbigg was not weeping for her dead child; she was crying for herself.

14

Another Diary

Down at Singleton Police Station Detective Ryan was reading another of Kathleen Folbigg's diaries. This one shook him to his core. It left no doubt in his mind that she was the killer of all four of her children. This 1997 diary was written six years later than the first diary and, to Detective Ryan's critical eye, was far more damning. Slowly, painfully, he began to decipher Kathleen Folbigg's appalling handwriting and realise the horror within. It was not simple; most entries revolved around her obsession with the gym, weight loss and her desire to be looked at by men. She frequently recorded the attempts of Craig to reignite the sexual spark in their relationship and how she simply had no urges in that direction. Some entries, however, rang alarm bells for the policeman. On 6 July 1997, before Laura was born, Kathy wrote about her life with Craig:

Maybe then he will see, when stress of it all is getting to be too much, and save me from feeling like I did before,

during my dark moods. Hopefully, preparing myself will
mean the end of my dark moods, or at least the ability to
see it coming, and say to him or someone, `Hey, help. I'm
getting overwhelmed here. Help me out.' That will be the key
to this baby's survival. It surely will. But enough dwelling.
Things are different this time. It will all work out for sure.

If Caleb, Patrick and Sarah had died from natural
causes why would their mother's dark moods affect
the survival of the next baby? Detective Ryan now
thought he knew the answer to that question. He read
on, pausing at the 11 June 1997 entry:

Don't think I'll suffer Alzheimer's disease. My brain has too
much happening, unstored and unrecalled memories, just
waiting. Heaven help the day they surface and I recall. That
will be the day to lock me up and throw away the key,
something I'm sure will happen one day.

Detective Ryan was also sure this would happen one
day. In fact, he was the one who had pledged to
himself that he would make it happen, especially in
light of the revelations in the diary he was now examining. He pondered on the entry Kathy had written on
26 June 1997:

This time I'm positive, with support from friends et cetera
and Craig, this time everything will work out fine and the

220

sight and visions of the future I've been having will come true this time. With the other three I never bothered to think of school and teenage years, maybe because I always knew they'd never get there. But this one I see myself taking her to school and Craig doing homework et cetera with her. Therefore, I assume I'm actually ready for the family life now, where I wasn't before. Feeling secure, loved, successful and wanted by Craig has helped me and, to a degree, the fact that I don't wish to die with no one really knowing I was here. At last, now I know my son or daughter will. If God or that elusive higher power doesn't take them away from me once they are older to punish me. I'm trying to do this right. I hope that is received and understood.

Clearly, thought the detective, she was not concerned that God would take the children away from her while they were young but when they were older. Surely a mother who had lost three babies under the age of one year would be more worried that she would lose them as babies. Not Kathleen Folbigg. And for that, Bernie Ryan could find only one explanation. Another entry before Laura was born also troubled him:

I accept that my identity as a person starts with me. I've decided that's the way it must be. I have no past, no relatives to remind me, and I am it, so therefore, the choice of this baby was to extend me, natural, and one I've made happily and wholeheartedly, and would make again, I'm sure. Problem was with the other three kids felt I didn't deserve to be extended, and that I was condemning them to life with me. That feeling has changed, so this time all is well and well it will go.

Laura Elizabeth Folbigg had been born on 7 August 1997. Eighteen days later, on 25 August 1997, Detective Ryan read the entry Kathy had confided to her diary after the birth of her daughter in which she admitted to herself the '*scary feelings*' that she had bonded with Laura and had a maternal instinct she had not felt with her other children. More tellingly, she also revealed that the constant downloads to the hospital from the monitor meant '*everything will be fine this time*'.

To Detective Ryan this meant only one thing – the monitor was keeping Kathy honest. The external checks by nurse Margaret Tanner at the sleep clinic meant she had to keep the monitor on Laura or else there would be questions. The downside, of course, was that the constant alarms from the monitor kept waking Kathy up. And she was not a woman who coped well without sleep. On 20 September 1997, just six weeks after the birth, he read about how irritable her lack of sleep was making her. She called it '*punishment for the others*'. The policeman could think of only one reason why she needed to be punished. And he noted the growing stress

Kathy was feeling as '*selfish prick*' Craig suggested he should sleep in the spare room because he needed to get enough sleep before work. Once again. Kathy told her diary she felt very alone. Detective Ryan believed that when she felt like that it meant it was only a matter of time before bad things started to happen.

On 3 November 1997 Kathy had clearly been down in the dumps and had written:

Why is it when I'm so tired, I'm feeling sick, shitty, I can't sleep, very depressed with myself at the moment, feeling deprived of my freedom. I know that's the price that you pay for having a baby, but I'd not be human if it didn't get me down a little every now and then. It's because my release and enjoyment of the gym's been taken away. I have to take her with me most times now, which means I can't enjoy myself and turn off like I usually do because she's there and I worry about her. Someone's awake. Got to go. Lost it with her earlier. Left her crying in the bedroom and had to walk out. That feeling was happening and I think it was because I had to clear my head and prioritise as I've done in here now. I love her, I really do. I don't want anything to happen.

The disintegrating state of the marriage was also evident by the diary entries. It was adding stress and pressure to an already tired Kathy. The person feeling the brunt of her anger was Laura. Her next entry on 9 November 1997 chillingly referred to Sarah's death:

Craig was pretty drunk Friday night. In his drunken stupor he admitted he is not really happy. There's a problem with his security level with me and he has a morbid fear about Laura. He – well I know there's nothing wrong with her, nothing out of the ordinary anyway. Because it was me, not them. Think I handle her fits of crying better than I did with Sarah. I've learned to, once getting to me, to walk away and breathe in for a while myself. It helps me cope and figure out how to help her. With Sarah all I wanted was her to shut up and one day she did.

If there was any doubt about what happened to the first three Folbigg children, to Detective Ryan that particular entry ended it. And with the pressure cooker of stress building up inside her mother, Laura's life was not looking too safe by this stage either.

As Detective Ryan read on, Kathy's stress was demonstrated more and more. On 8 December 1997 she had written:

Had a bad day today. Lost it with Laura a couple of times. She cried most of the day. Why do I do that? Must learn to read her better. She is pretty straightforward. She either wants to sleep or doesn't. Got to stop placing so much importance on myself. Must try to release my stress somehow. I'm starting to take it out on her. Bad move. Bad things and thoughts happen when that happens. It will never happen again.

Bernie Ryan could see from Kathy's diary that the writing was on the wall for Laura. He read of the first serious danger signal Kathy had recorded on 20 January 1998:

> The gym was a pivotal part of me and now, because I can't go without taking Laura, it's put a damper on everything. I've had my one and only escape taken away from me.

Then, a week later, the consequence of Kathy not having a form of stress release was clearly evident as told by her diary entry of 28 January 1998 when she admitted she had '*lost it*' with her daughter when she would not stop crying. At least Kathy had restrained herself and walked away. But she was well aware of what might happen to Laura:

> Scared that she'll leave me now like Sarah did. I knew I was short tempered and cruel sometimes to her and she left with a bit of help. I don't want that to ever happen again. I actually seem to have a bond with Laura. It can't happen again.

On 6 March 1998 Kathy had written again of her irritability:

> Laura not well. Really got on my nerves today. Snapped and got really angry, but not nearly as bad as I used to get.

The diaries continued in the same vein, only the instances of anger and frustration were drawing closer together. No single entry up until Laura's death a year later stood out particularly; rather it was the weight and cumulative effect of Kathy's anger and frustration that gave the policeman the overview that things had gone downhill during the last year of Laura's life. Leaning back on his chair with the diary still in his hand, Detective Ryan also reflected that Laura had been ill with a cold in the week before she died. A year before her death her mother had recorded the frustration she felt when the child was ill. There was no doubt in Detective Ryan's mind that Laura had been smothered for those same reasons. Sitting there in his office, he believed, particularly in light of this second diary, that he had a very strong case against Kathy.

Over the coming months Detective Ryan carefully put his brief together. He travelled to Canberra and Adelaide to meet with Australia's leading experts on SIDS. It took time and involved painstaking research but by late 2000 he was ready to send the brief off to the Department of Public Prosecutions (the DPP) so they could evaluate the evidence and recommend whether it was strong enough to secure a conviction.

Now all he could do was wait. It was an agonisingly slow process, but finally an answer was delivered to him.

No.

The DPP had assessed that there was insufficient evidence to prosecute and instead suggested that the deaths of the four children become the subject of a coronial inquest. The young detective felt incredibly let down, especially because so many people he had consulted – local and overseas experts, as well as other police – had given so much of themselves to help him in the pursuit of the truth about the death of the Folbigg children. Detective Ryan was devastated.

There was another option though. The DPP's decision was guidance. In most cases it was followed. But Detective Ryan could risk his reputation by ignoring the advice of the DPP and proceed with charging Kathleen Folbigg with the four murders. It was a big call.

Feeling that he was merely a country cop, with no experience in murder cases, the young detective felt that he lacked the courage to take such a step.

Instead he sent the brief off to the then Deputy State Coroner, Jan Stephenson, and asked for her opinion. Her view was more to his liking but still not what he hoped for. She told him that on her reading of the brief there was only enough evidence to charge Kathleen Folbigg with one murder, possibly Laura's.

He asked himself whether he should give up. He

certainly felt defeated but he was nothing if not tenacious. One murder charge was simply not good enough for him and he was not about to give away all of his hard work. He was convinced that Kathleen Folbigg had killed all four of her children. This time he telephoned a close friend, a prominent legal expert, who listened and finally said the words he longed to hear about charging Kathy with murder. 'Bernie, what's your problem? There's enough there. Why don't you just do it?'

If he turned away now a woman he believed to be a killer would get away with four murders. Those innocent babies would never receive justice. More than that, Kathleen Folbigg would be free to have more children and kill again.

He went home and talked to his best friend – his wife and the mother of their two daughters. Together they agonised over the details again. Bernie worried. Did he have enough evidence? Certainly the experts did not think so. It was his career and credibility on the line. He tossed and turned during the next few sleepless nights. His wife was fully supportive of him proceeding with the charges. She knew, as did her husband, that sometimes in life you cannot just walk away. Those children needed someone to fight for them. Kathleen Folbigg's future children needed someone to fight for them too. Like it or not, Bernie Ryan knew he was that man. Alone and out on a limb, he put everything on the line and decided to charge Kathleen Folbigg with the murder of her four babies.

15

Arrest

In June 2000 Kathy and Craig Folbigg had separated for good. Even though they had reconciled following Craig's return in May 1999 to the police station to 'soften' his statement about his suspicions concerning his wife, their relationship had gone dramatically downhill after the police had interviewed her. Craig felt Kathy was too domineering in the way she berated him about how weak she thought he was because he was still pining over their children. Kathy felt her husband would not move on. Once again, the couple was moving apart. Kathy went back to the gym and back to work. Craig continued to feel terrible.

Detective Ryan knew the couple had split up. He was keeping a close eye on the couple and was talking to Craig. Once he had made the decision to arrest Kathy another problem presented itself. Craig's changed statement of May 1999 was not the truth and Detective Ryan knew it. That statement weakened his case. He needed Craig to tell the truth. Certainly Craig should be more amenable to it now that Kathy had split up with him again. The policeman wanted to be sure. On 19 April 2001 Detective Ryan scared the living daylights out of Craig Folbigg. He placed him under arrest.

Detective Ryan and Detective Senior Constable Frith presented a very formidable front when they turned up at Craig's office at Teasdales car dealership, informed him that he was under arrest and escorted him to their waiting police car. As Craig was driven to Singleton Police Station he was told that he was to be charged with hindering an investigation.

The car salesman was terrified. He realised that Detective Ryan knew that he had lied when he changed his statement nearly two years before. His mind was racing. The ramifications of the charge were very serious and frightening to a man who had not been on the wrong side of the law before. He feared it meant people would think he was a criminal. Even more, he feared the possibility of jail. He did not know exactly what the charge of hindering an investigation meant, but he did know he was now in a very dire situation.

At the police station, Craig was led to a room where Detective Ryan once again commenced conducting an interview recorded on both audio- and videotapes. Only this time, just as the policeman hoped, fear had brought about a remarkable change in Craig Folbigg's attitude. This time there was no repeat of his attempts to soften the answers he had given when interviewed by Detective Ryan for the very first time. Craig now told the truth to the best of his ability.

The last loose end was tied up and Detective Ryan now did what he had been waiting to do for so long, and after so much hard work. That afternoon he drove to Kathy Folbigg's new home in Boonal Street, Singleton, and placed her under arrest. She was taken to Singleton Police Station where she was formally charged with the murder of Caleb, Patrick, Sarah and Laura Folbigg. Her own babies.

The next day, 20 April 2001, Kathleen Megan Folbigg, then aged 33, appeared in Muswellbrook Local Court to face four counts of murder. The prosecutor, Sergeant Dave Barron, said the case would rely on evidence from Kathy's estranged husband, Craig, excerpts from her diaries, and evidence from pathology experts in England and the United States.

'In all the cases the defendant was the person who located the kids. In all the cases it was a short time after death and the bodies were still warm. There has been expert evidence obtained from Australia and overseas as far as the method or cause of the deaths. All deaths were caused by smothering and all deaths are homicides,' said Sergeant Barron to the magistrate.

The magistrate, Ian Guy, refused Kathy bail. She was remanded to Mulawa Women's Prison and held under strict security until her appearance in Maitland Local Court the following Monday.

Local papers carried the story on the front page. Unfortunately for some of them, the photograph they had obtained from Kathy's colleagues at Retravision incorrectly identified another woman as the accused child killer. Profuse apologies to the woman mistakenly identified as Kathleen Folbigg were printed in the papers the next day.

When Kathy was arrested there was one man who was badly shaken up by it – her new boyfriend of the last 10 months – 35-year-old Tony Lambkin. Kathy had moved on quickly after the breakdown of her marriage and the Singleton builder was so head over heels in love with Kathy that he wanted to marry her. Communication between the two, however, could have been better. He had known nothing of the police investigation until many months after they had started going out together.

They had met at the BodyFlex gym in Singleton soon after Kathy and Craig had split. Tony had been completing some renovations for his brother, who owned the gym and while he was there his sister introduced him to Kathy. They were instantly attracted to one another and arranged a first date at the local bowling club.

With Kathy, Tony felt all his dreams had finally come true because he had never felt so in love.

However he knew all was not well with his new love because at times she would cry all night and sometimes still be in tears the next morning.

Later in the relationship she finally told him what the problem was, just before they were about to move in together. Kathy suddenly turned around in bed one night and said: 'Tony, there's something hanging over my head . . . and I need to talk to you about it. I've been accused of killing my four children.'

Tony was in complete shock because up until then he had not even been aware that she had ever had kids. Kathy explained to him they had all died from SIDS and that her husband had turned on her after they had split and that the case was now in the hands of the police. As Kathy wept, she explained that despite Craig and the police being wrong, she had no idea what would happen.

Tony could not understand the charges. Kathy was the most gentle and caring person he had ever met and he knew she loved children and wanted more. His children.

'She has suffered a hard life and is pretty much alone in this world. But she has so much love to give and all she ever wanted in return was to be loved,' he later said.

On 24 April 2001 Kathy was driven from Mulawa Women's Prison to Maitland Local Court where her solicitor, Brian Doyle, made an application for bail. 'Any way you look at it, the police case is a weak one with no direct evidence whatsoever,' he said.

Tony Lambkin sat at the back of the court. Mr Doyle told the court that Kathy and the builder had been dating since August and that he had recently proposed to her. 'He asked her to marry him but she hasn't been able to say yes because of this being over her head for two years.' Tony Lambkin was prepared to act as surety in order to get bail for his lover while she awaited trial.

Police prosecutor Sergeant Daniel Maher brought up the evidence of Dr Janice Ophoven in requesting that bail be denied. 'There is a strong case on the report by the doctor who found the odds of four unexplained infant deaths occurring in one family with children under two years was one in a trillion,' he said. 'It would mean this was the only case ever occurring in the world. That is just not likely.'

Bail was refused. As she was led to the prison van outside the court, a devastated Kathy had only one word for the assembled media pack. 'Innocent,' she said.

One month after her arrest, Kathy appeared before New South Wales Supreme Court Justice Robert Hulme on 18 May 2001 in prison greens to again request bail in order to prepare to fight the substantial Crown case against her.

Detective Ryan was not happy about the possibility of Kathy being released on bail. 'I have grave concerns that [she] will attempt to manipulate her estranged husband into changing his evidence in relation to this matter,' he said. And Crown prosecutor Matt Laffan opposed the bail because she was a severe flight risk who had nothing to lose by running away.

Kathy completely denied having anything to do with the deaths of her children and told the court she wanted to go home and live with her boyfriend, Mr Lambkin, and resume her job waitressing at the local hotel.

Justice Hulme weighed up the arguments presented before him and decided she had a right to adequately prepare her legal defence. 'On the material before me, I would describe the Crown case as not lower than substantial. The evidence is that she has no more children and there is nothing to suggest that [she] has ever been a danger to anyone else.'

Kathy was released on $8000 bail provided she live with Tony Lambkin, report to the police twice a week, not apply for a passport or go within three kilometres of airports or international departure points. She was also instructed not to contact any Crown witnesses.

Tony Lambkin underwrote her bail by posting a $4000 surety for her.

Life awaiting trial is a type of limbo. Tony and Kathy lived together, went through the motions of normal life, all the time waiting for the agonisingly slow legal process to move on. A year had passed by the time Tony Lambkin escorted Kathy to Newcastle Local Court on 25 May 2002. Kathy stood in the dock in a green pants-suit and cream shirt while the prosecution set out its case. Kathy's solicitor, Brian Doyle, had argued that the diary entries could be read in a way other than the one Detective Ryan believed. 'They could be the view of a mother tortured in the face of other children having died and blaming her own motherly inadequacies for the death, not her own actions.' Magistrate Alan Railton compared the case to that of Lindy Chamberlain. The magistrate told the court that the case was circumstantial and that the evidence was very emotive because babies were involved. He decided to suppress diary entries, excerpts from the listening devices and the expert medical opinions as he did not want the public to hear them. 'We have seen terrible injustices that can flow from public attention in respect to Lindy Chamberlain and it would be a tragedy if it happened in this case.' The magistrate committed Kathy to stand trial in the Supreme Court in 2003.

Certainly that was the view held by Tony Lambkin. He had spent the past year, in the looming shadow of the court case, falling deeper and deeper in love with Kathy. She would not commit to him because of the case but he respected her even more because of that.

They eventually shared two years together before Kathy's Supreme Court trial in Sydney in May 2003. However, it was very difficult for Kathy to sustain her relationship because of her public notoriety. Every time they stepped out in public, people would recognise and point at her, both in Singleton and in Newcastle. Tony and Kathy felt it was as though everyone had already made up their minds she was guilty of murdering her children, before the case had even gone to trial.

The pressure became too much and Kathy ended the relationship to spare Tony the agony she was about to go through. Tony later said: 'She realised the whole of Australia would know who she was by the time the trial had finished and she didn't want that for me. Maybe she was even worried I wouldn't stand by her; that I'd just slip away like everything else had in her life.'

Kathy moved in with a friend named Kylie, taking her cat, Boof, with her. She was confident that at the end of the trial she would be able to pick the cat up from her friend and resume her life in Singleton. Tony Lambkin was also waiting for her to return to him after the trial.

Apart from Tony, Kathy's other confidante had been her foster sister, Lea. Kathy knew she could trust and talk to her sister after hearing Lea's anger at the police 'witch-hunt'. However, her trust was misplaced.

Over time, visits and phone calls by Detective Ryan had convinced Lea that her sister had killed the children. For at least a year before the trial, Lea recorded every telephone conversation she had with Kathy and reported it all back to Detective Ryan. For Kathy this would prove to be a devastating betrayal.

In 1999 Lea had been interviewed by the police from Singleton but did not mention any of her suspicions. Of her first interview by the police she later said: 'I did not lie. I just did not say everything . . . it was a total witch-hunt and I was very angry at them even thinking that of Kathy.'

She wanted to protect her little sister and made sure she painted a rosy picture of her character to the police. 'I could not and would not have anybody saying things about my sister; there was just no way,' said Lea.

Detective Ryan travelled to Melbourne and had several meetings with Lea over the coming months. He not only convinced her that he was not conducting a witch-hunt; he helped persuade her of her sister's guilt by explaining the expert evidence he had gathered.

After Detective Ryan's visits to her in Melbourne Lea began to think again about Kathy's behaviour with her children. Seeds of doubt had first been sown in her mind when she, her husband, their son and his then girlfriend travelled to Singleton to stay with Kathy and Craig for the memorial service of Lea's father and Kathy's foster father, Neville Marlborough, in January 1998. Laura had been five months old and on the apnoea monitor.

One afternoon everyone was gathered around the pool in the back garden, apart from Laura who was asleep in her room. Lea was suffering from a migraine and went inside to lie down. She had only just started to drift off when there was a loud, high-pitched noise like the fire detectors in the house. There was no reaction from anybody outside despite the alarm going off twice. Lea later mentioned it to Kathy who told her casually that it was probably the baby monitor and that she had not heard it.

Then there was the time Kathy and Craig took 17-month-old Laura to Lea's house for a holiday over Christmas 1998. Kathy and Lea were very close at the time and Laura was very special to Lea; Lea considered her the granddaughter she had always wanted.

As the week progressed, Lea noticed her sister was getting tired because of the sleeping arrangements. 'We had a pull-out bed in the spare room, which had a bar going across, it wasn't very comfortable and we had a cot for Laura. Laura would toss around a bit so she wasn't sleeping too good so Kathy and Craig would then put Laura in bed with them so they would end up putting the mattress down on the floor to allow them to get some sleep and Kathy wasn't getting much sleep at all,' Lea later recalled.

The lack of sleep put Kathy in a bad mood and Lea saw for herself exactly what her foster sister's temper was like. 'Kathy lost her temper with Laura when she was trying to feed her in the high chair,' she said. 'Laura didn't really want to eat her meal and Kathy got angry with her and put the food down . . . on the dining-room table and got Laura out, pulled Laura out by the arm. She just got her by the arm that way and yanked her out . . . Angry because Laura wouldn't eat.'

Lea felt Kathy's anger was completely unwarranted. 'Because Laura didn't want to eat, which is normal of a child that age, and instead of forcing, if Laura had just been left and allowed to eat when she was ready to eat, she would have been okay, but Kathy just insisted that she was to eat when [Kathy] said that she had to eat and Kathy just lost it with her. I turned and gave her a filthy look and Kathy turned around and calmed right down.'

Kathy's flash of temper had shocked Lea and the memory of it would always remain with her. Matters got worse on Christmas Eve. 'Laura didn't want to go to bed because there was a lot of excitement going around in the house with people coming to see us for Christmas and that, and Laura didn't want to go down to sleep and when Kathy tried to put her down she still didn't want to get down and Kathy got angry,' said Lea.

She felt Kathy went 'over the top' with her anger. 'I just didn't feel it was necessary to have been so angry with her considering Laura's age . . . it is typical of a little girl of that age . . . There's a lot of excitement going on.'

Detective Ryan's dogged determination in convincing Lea of Kathy's guilt paid off. Lea made a statement to him about the conversation she had with Kathy about the night Sarah died. This evidence was to form a crucial plank in the case against Kathy because Craig said that she had been out of bed with Sarah at 1.10am with the light on. This contradicted Kathy's version of events. When Lea spoke to police she recalled the conversation from years before. 'Kathy told me that Sarah . . . had woken, that Sarah had been put to bed next to her because it was easier for her to just find the dummy and put it into Sarah's mouth during the night instead of having to get up and go into the other bedroom. She said she got up that night, went to the toilet and either put the hall light on or the toilet light, I am not 100 per cent sure which light it was, and from seeing from the toilet she could see there was something with [Sarah] . . . there was something wrong with her and she looked a greyish colour. She said from the toilet she sang out to Craig, Craig didn't answer, she sang out again, Craig didn't answer and she screamed out a third time and ran in and Craig woke up and found [Sarah] and tried to do what he could with CPR, which he didn't know much of at that time.'

After Lea made her statement she spoke to Kathy on the telephone. Kathy asked her how it had gone and when Lea recalled the part about Sarah's death Kathy became very angry.

'That is not how Sarah died,' Kathy told her sister. 'Anyway, there was no light on.'

By the time of this conversation Lea was a convert to Detective Ryan's cause. She would record and relay back to him every conversation she had with Kathy. She recalled to him how in 1999 Kathy had bragged to her about the way she had disciplined her puppy, Basil. 'Kath rang me up and bragged how she'd kicked him down the stairs for weeing on the floor and wouldn't come to her when she said so,' said Lea.

Lea's regular taped conversations with her foster sister involved Kathy telling her how well her defence case was going and what she was going to do with all the money once she sold her story.

'Kath's been talking about money all the time and how much money she's going to make. You just want to put your hands down the phone and choke her. She said her girlfriend wanted her to buy her a cappuccino machine and she was going to have a Queensland holiday.'

These conversations helped convince Lea of her sister's guilt. To maintain frequent contact with Kathy so as to keep the phone calls going, Lea bit her tongue rather than tackle Kathy about her behaviour and inconsistencies and risk her cutting all contact. In February 2003 Kathy discovered Lea was actually a key witness for the prosecution. She felt she had been betrayed and so cut all contact with her sister. Lea could not bear to wipe Kathy's last voicemail message to her from her answerphone. Despite what Lea believed Kathy had done, she would never stop loving her as her little sister.

'Why did she have to take the children? Why didn't she ask for help? Why did she keep having more?' Lea wondered.

Many sleepless nights brought Lea to the conclusion that Kathy enjoyed the attention of being pregnant and having a new baby, but when the realities of caring for a baby 24 hours a day, every day, became quickly apparent, the children became a burden because they interfered with her social life.

More tellingly, during all those phone calls, her sister observed that Kathy had never once protested her innocence. 'She never once said to me, "Lea, I didn't do this"; never ever once did she say that.' As a result, Lea is convinced that her sister murdered her own babies.

Lea was reported in a newspaper as saying that she felt Kathy should get the death penalty and that if this were possible she would be the first one to line up to inject her.

During Kathy's trial, as Lea sat in the witness box and gave evidence against her sister for the prosecution, Kathy did not look up at her once.

16
Trial

Court Two of the New South Wales Supreme Court at Darlinghurst is in an ugly modern building around the corner from the original sandstone courthouse in Taylor Square at the grimy end of Sydney's Oxford Street. Craig Folbigg arrived there on Tuesday 1 April 2003 for the murder trial of his estranged wife. He had his large family in tow, offering him solidarity and support. His sisters Jan and Carol and brother Michael would be constantly at his side, as would his new girlfriend. Young real-estate valuer Helen Pearce was stoic in her support. Every day they stood – most of them smoking – on the steps of the court, meeting with Detective Ryan, who also attended every day of the seven-week trial, and would talk to Kathy's sister, Lea, and mother, Deirdre Marlborough, who travelled down from Darwin to attend the trial for a few days.

In stark contrast, Kathy was very much alone. She was on bail and had asked the Salvation Army to find her a family she could stay with for the duration of the trial. Two couples from Singleton came to offer her brief support but her only constant friend and confidante during the lunch and tea breaks of the seven-week trial was the Salvation Army's court chaplain, Major Joyce Harmer. They would sit together in a tiny room off the court foyer to avoid the newspaper, television and radio journalists and photographers milling around outside. There was a great deal of public interest in the case. It seemed everyone in Australia at the time had an opinion and wanted to know more.

Detective Ryan was there every day without fail. Such was his personal involvement in the trial that he even brought his wife down for a few days to sit in and watch.

Kathy's case fell under the benign gaze of the grey-haired and bearded Justice Graham Barr who proved himself to be decisive with the lawyers and unfailingly considerate and concerned for the welfare of the six-man, six-woman jury, which had to reach a majority verdict on the charges facing Kathleen Folbigg – the stony-faced, red-haired, well-groomed 35-year-old sitting just five paces from them in the wooden dock.

Opening the prosecution case was New South Wales's star Crown prosecutor, Mark Tedeschi QC. The 51-year-old married father of three had already prosecuted a number of high-profile cases. Backpacker killer Ivan Milat and Cabramatta MP John Newman's killer Phung Ngo were both behind bars after his successful prosecutions. He had also been involved in two trials over the Sydney Hilton Hotel bombing, prosecuted notorious underworld figure Neddy Smith for the murder of a tow-truck driver in Coogee, and in the case of the murder of renowned heart surgeon Victor Chang prosecuted his killers. Even 'Golden Tonsils' radio host John Laws had come up against the Queens Counsel for breaching the Jury Act by approaching a juror for an interview. A slight, engaging and mild-mannered man with brilliant courtroom technique, he was more than qualified to take on the Kathleen Folbigg case. He showed his consummate professionalism by delivering his complex closing address the day after his mother died from a long-standing illness. Supporting him was New South Wales's newest Crown prosecutor, herself a rising star, Jane Culver, and solicitor Laurel Baglee.

Once the jury was sworn in, Mr Tedeschi began. 'Ladies and gentlemen, the Crown representing the community of New South Wales brings these charges against the accused, Kathleen Folbigg. And because the Crown brings the charges, it is the Crown that has the burden of proving these charges. The accused doesn't have to prove anything.'

The five charges were: 1) On 20 February 1989 at Mayfield in the State of New South Wales she did murder Caleb Gibson Folbigg. 2) On 18 October 1990 at Mayfield in the State of New South Wales she did maliciously inflict grievous bodily harm to Patrick Allen Folbigg with intent to do grievous bodily harm. 3) On 13 February 1991 at Mayfield in the State of New South Wales did murder Patrick Allen Folbigg. 4) On 30 August 1993 at Thornton in the State of New South Wales did murder Sarah Kathleen Folbigg. 5) On 1 March 1999 at Singleton in the State of New South Wales did murder Laura Elizabeth Folbigg.

Kathy pleaded not guilty to all of them.

'There are murder charges in relation to each of the four children. Now, basically, the Crown alleges that the accused murdered each of her four baby children over the course of about ten years, one at a time. She only had one child at a time. It is alleged that she murdered each of them. It is also alleged, in relation to Patrick, and this is charge number two, that she attempted to smother the child, but that the child was revived by ambulance officers in hospital and didn't die on that occasion, but died some months later,' said Mr Tedeschi to the jury.

The Crown did not have to prove her motive for smothering each of the children but Mr Tedeschi offered an explanation. 'The accused had a very low threshold for stress, and she was also deeply resentful at the intrusions that her children made on her own life and, in particular, on her sleep, her ability to go to the gym, and her ability to socialise, including going out dancing.

'She was constantly tired, resentful against her

husband, Craig, for not providing her with what she considered to be adequate help, and she was constantly, we say, constantly preoccupied, to an exaggerated degree, with her weight gain due, in part, to the fact that she couldn't get to the gym as much as she liked because of her children.

'The Crown case is that she either intended to kill them during a flash of anger, resentment and hatred against her children, or, alternatively, that she deliberately sought to render them unconscious in an attempt to put them to sleep, either so that she could get to sleep herself or that she could have some time to herself.'

The Crown prosecutor then went into the detail of each child's death before bringing up Kathy's diaries. 'These diaries, the Crown case is, were written totally for herself and for no one else. They were written often at the end of the day when she was in bed just before sleep. Sometimes they are almost intelligible. Many hours have gone into deciphering them. They contain details of her most personal thoughts about her intimate private life with Craig, which are not tendered to titillate anybody, but are tendered to show that this was a very serious diary with her innermost thoughts about the most intimate subjects. They deal with her frustrations with her weight gain, the frustrations with the restrictions the babies placed on her life . . . her tiredness, her moods, her lack of toleration for her babies and her inability to control her actions with her babies. They deal with the hope she will be able to control herself.'

Mr Tedeschi's next step was to read out the diary entries to the jury. He knew how much effort had gone into translating them because he had also spent hours himself doing it. One entry that he had managed to decipher was particularly devastating. The Crown prosecutor would later go to great lengths to show that Kathy had been to visit a clairvoyant with Craig's sister Carol 'Kaz' Newitt. He read several entries but before he read the entry for 15 December 1997 he explained to the jury: 'You will recall from a previous entry that Kathleen Folbigg had been to see a clairvoyant. The Crown case is from that entry, and from other things that she wrote that I will not read to you, she believed in reincarnation. She believed that the souls of her deceased children were there for clairvoyants who had special abilities to be able to contact [them]. She believed that Laura had a life in the other world before being born.' He read out the entry:

Kaz sent a beautiful angel and teddy for Laura. Both her and Craig are convinced that Laura's soul is not her own. By the looks of it. Me, well, I'm sure she met everyone and they've told her 'don't be a bad or sickly kid. Mum may, you know, crack it'. They've warned her. Good. But she is still her own little person and will always be. Must stop calling her Sarah. She's most definitely not her.

Mr Tedeschi outlined the Crown's interpretation of this diary entry. 'The Crown case is that she believed that the reason why Laura was such a good child was because the previous three children who had been killed by her had warned Laura to be a good child so that the same fate would not befall her.'

He also read out the thoughts she had recorded on 31 December 1997:

> Getting Laura to be [one] next year ought to be fun. She'll realise a party is going on and that will be it. Wonder if the battle of the wills will start with her and I then? We'll actually get to see. She is a fairly good-natured baby. Thank goodness. It will save her from the fate of her siblings. I think she was warned.

He concluded by telling the jury: 'Ladies and gentlemen, the Crown says that this is not a case where you will hear any evidence in the Crown case to suggest that the accused Kathleen Folbigg had any mental illness such as post-natal depression, or Munchausen syndrome by proxy or any other mental illness. Kathleen Folbigg did not kill or injure her children to get attention for herself or in a state of profound depression. The Crown says she killed them because she couldn't stand their crying and the demands that they made on her life.'

Mr Tedeschi claimed the jury would be reading the

diaries for themselves, seeing a video interview with Kathy and hearing from a number of expert witnesses. 'That, ladies and gentlemen, concludes the opening address of the Crown.'

Sitting at the lawyers' table with the Crown team was Kathy's defence team, headed by 47-year-old father-of-three Senior Counsel Peter Zahra, the Senior Public Defender of New South Wales, a religious and committed lawyer well known for his extreme concern for his clients. He had already spent his career working on some of the biggest cases in Australian history. He had defended Craig Andrew Merritt, the father sentenced to life in prison for smothering his three children to death on Father's Day 2001, paedophile Michael Guider who pleaded guilty to the manslaughter of Sydney schoolgirl Samantha Knight back in 1986, and had successfully defended a 12-year-old boy, the youngest ever to be charged with manslaughter, against allegations he had drowned six-year-old Corey Davis in March 1998. Despite these cases being well known in Australia, Mr Zahra had kept a low public profile by slipping into court by the back door to avoid the media spotlight. However, it was difficult to escape the media's attention in this case because of the intense interest in the Folbigg trial. There was only one door into the court he could use so he had to walk past the cameras every day. Up until that point, he had managed to keep such a low profile during his career that other parents at his children's soccer games on a Saturday morning had thought he was a builder.

His learned junior, Public Defender Anthony Cook, and Kathy's Legal Aid Commission solicitor, Peter Krisenthal, who sat just in front of her, would often lean over to confer with her in the dock during the trial.

Peter Zahra rose to his feet to tell the jury that he did not propose to go through all the evidence as the Crown had just done but would allow the trial to unfold. He told the jury that the truth of the case would be found in the detail of each child's death and not with a sweeping overview. 'This is not a case which lends itself to a broad brush to just look at the big picture. It is important to recognise that that is not the only step. The step of then looking at the cases individually is, in fact, the most important part of your determination.'

In fact, the defence had wanted to have a separate murder trial for each child so that each jury would not know about the deaths of the other siblings. Right up until the trial – and through it – the defence team literally spent many, many sleepless nights making phone calls to experts across the globe in their quest for new medical evidence. At the heart of the defence-team efforts was the search for medical research that would offer a genetic reason for why the babies had died. Cutting-edge research released by the Mayo Clinic in the United States indicated there could be a genetic link between SIDS deaths and the serotonin gene that could explain four deaths in the one family. The defence team left no stone unturned in gathering medical evidence and they had a number of laboratories around the world assisting them. The trial was delayed, firstly with an attempt to get separate trials for each of the children, and then to wait for the medical evidence that would give a genetic explanation for their deaths.

Mr Zahra told the jury there was a medical explanation for each of the children's deaths. Caleb had a floppy larynx, Patrick suffered from epilepsy, Sarah's uvula was congested and Laura had myocarditis. 'None of the experts and particularly the pathologists who carried out the post-mortems could find any evidence to support positively that this was suffocation,' he said. 'There will be nothing, no evidence during the course of this trial that there was, in fact, a history of physical abuse to any of these children at the hands of the accused.'

He told the jury that the Crown's allegations were incongruous and did not fit Kathy's profile. 'This is not a situation where people will come to court and even say "I saw her slap the child". No evidence is expected to be called about that.'

He asked the jury to draw on their own experiences

when considering the diary entries and question whether they were literal explanations of what happened or indicative of Kathy's state of mind at the time of writing. 'This is a diary. We draw from our experiences in life and no doubt it may not necessarily follow that there is, in fact, a basis upon which to read every world literally as being indicative of a description of what, in fact, happened or what was, in fact, her true state of mind.

'There may, in fact, be some basis upon which we might understand the diaries in the context of experiencing the deaths of the children as going through some fairly normal human reactions, not only of grief, maybe feelings of shame, feelings of guilt, feelings of responsibility. Asking the "what if?" questions.'

He concluded his opening address by reminding the jury that it was not up to Kathleen Folbigg to prove that the children died of natural causes; it was up to the Crown to prove beyond reasonable doubt that she killed them.

First on the stand was Craig Folbigg. His evidence was hugely emotional. Several times he broke down and cried for his dead children. Over the course of several days he painted a picture for the court of life with Kathy. At one stage the courtroom doors shook as he mimicked the growl Kathy would let out when she was frustrated. Throughout it all, Kathy remained resolute, without a glimmer of emotion.

Every day the Salvation Army court chaplain, Major Joyce Harmer, sat in court in the same spot so that she could see Kathy's facial expressions and provide her with a friendly face to turn to if needed. She could also see Craig and the rest of the family and offer them support if they needed it. 'They were very glad I was supporting her. They said: "Joyce, she needs you."'

And they were right. 'There were patches of devastation and at that point in time I believe . . . Kath needed a hug and I sensed that she just needed to be hugged. And I would hug her and she would hug me and I believe that that has its own kind of interpretation of care and concern.'

In fact, she felt Kathy was 'just like any other woman walking down the street'. She and her husband had taken her to Kiama on one of the weekend adjournments to get Kathy out for a break and they had all eaten ice-creams and had a perfectly normal afternoon out. 'I became her friend and I felt the need to be just that. That's what my work is about – being close by people who are distressed and devastated and sometimes can't think for themselves. So I think for them.'

'I would escort her out of court every day and if there was something that she didn't agree with that was said, she would express that to me. She would often say: 'Did you hear so and so? That didn't really happen.'

'She would sit on the desk and swing her legs. We would talk about the rain and what we were having for lunch or how Kathy had slept that night,' said Major Harmer.

Kathy took a very active interest in the comings and goings of the people involved in the court process. She would ask Major Harmer the identity of all the people in the court that she did not know. There was a daily media presence. 'She said she didn't hate the media . . . they were just doing their job,' said Major Harmer.

Although in the initial stages of the trial it was hard to judge Kathy's emotional state from her detached demeanour, Lea Bown told reporters it was possible to tell Kathy's mood by the colour of her hair. When it was blonde she was upbeat and bubbly. For the trial it was red. Every day she appeared immaculately coiffured, usually in a blue suit, betraying no sign of what was happening inside.

The first chink in Kathy's armour came during the testimony of pathologist Dr Cala. A video of Laura's last day alive was played to the court to show how healthy she had been. The vivacious little girl wearing the orange floaties in the backyard pool was a blonde-haired delight. Less than 24 hours after that video was made she was dead. In court, her mother put her head in her hands and sobbed.

Kathy herself did not give evidence. The nearest the jury came to hearing her speak was in the video-taped interview she had had with Detective Bernie Ryan on 23 July 1999. She sat in court, in the dock, as the tape was played, watching herself answering questions that would haunt her for the rest of her life.

On tape Detective Ryan asked her: 'Can you close your eyes and see the face of all four of your children?'

Kathy answered: 'I honestly tell you now I can see Laura's clearly; Sarah's, Patrick's and Caleb's take photographs for me to remember what they looked like. Basic features I can tell you.'

Detective Ryan: 'How do you feel for those children?'

Kathy: 'For them, or how do I feel for myself?'

Detective Ryan: 'How do you feel for them?'

Kathy: 'That they are somewhere peaceful, happy.'

Detective Ryan: 'Do you really believe that?'

Kathy: 'I don't know, I don't know, I prefer to believe that. That's probably what it is.'

By now, in court, Kathy had started to cry as she continued to listen to the answers she had given to Detective Ryan's questions.

Detective Ryan: 'Do you think Craig is responsible for the deaths of your children?'

Kathy: 'No.'

Detective Ryan: 'Do you know what sort of person would kill four children?'

Kathy: 'I have no comprehension and I don't even want to think about it.'

Detective Ryan: 'Are you responsible for the death of Caleb?'

Kathy: 'No.'

In court, Kathy cried out in anguish. Behind her, in the public gallery, Craig and his sister Carol were also crying and holding on to each other. Tissues were passed around. The tape kept rolling.

Detective Ryan: 'Are you responsible for the death of Patrick?'

Kathy: 'No, no.'

Detective Ryan: 'Are you responsible for the death of Sarah?'

Kathy: 'No.'

Detective Ryan: 'Are you responsible for the death of Laura?'

Kathy: 'No.'

Detective Ryan: 'Kathy, did you kill Caleb?'

Kathy: 'NO!!!'

Detective Ryan: 'Did you kill Patrick?'

Kathy: 'No.'

Detective Ryan: 'Did you try to kill Patrick on that near-miss episode?'

Kathy: 'No.'

Detective Ryan: 'Did you kill Sarah?'

Kathy: 'No.'

Detective Ryan: 'And did you kill Laura?'

Kathy: 'No.'

Distraught, Kathy sat with her forehead resting on the wooden dock. Shaking all over, she stood and started to stumble out of the dock. Justice Barr shouted for her to stop as she reached the public gallery. Kathy was hysterical. Major Harmer from the Salvation Army rushed to her aid and the judge was forced to adjourn the trial for the day as Kathy was taken to nearby St Vincent's Hospital and sedated.

She appeared in court the next day with a chalky pallor to her skin and still looking badly shaken. The legal process ground on.

The prosecution case lasted several weeks and brought in experts from overseas whom Detective Ryan had met on his investigative odyssey, and also friends and family of Kathy and Craig. By contrast, the defence case lasted just three days because expert testimony from overseas it had been relying upon was simply not yet available. The witnesses for the defence comprised Kathy's friends from the gym – Jan Bull, Debbie Goodchild and Judith Patterson – and two medical experts. Under cross-examination Kathy's gym friends were found to have shared no close confidences with Kathy about the state of her marriage. The prosecution attempted to show that this indicated they were not close enough to the real Kathy of the diaries for their opinions to be worthwhile.

The trial took an enormous toll on the defence

team. Each cross-examination of the medical experts for the prosecution involved telephone calls to their own experts around the world and yet more sleepless nights. 'The burden here was the complexity of the evidence. You can imagine the work that was done there,' Peter Zahra said after the trial. Even in the cross-examination of Craig Folbigg, Mr Zahra later said that Craig's 'gymnastics' in response to questions from the defence team – because of the amendments he had made to his initial police statement – was the result of questions based on hours and hours of work studying tapes recorded from the listening devices.

Professor Roger Byard from the Forensic Science Centre in Adelaide, a pathologist who had received a number of awards for his work on SIDS, provided the cornerstone of Kathy's defence. In particular, with respect to Laura he argued that myocarditis could not be excluded as a possible cause of death. In court he was given a very thorough cross-examination, which culminated in the question:

'Professor, just before the jury went out you agreed that it was not a reasonable conclusion that these children could all have died from the same natural cause. Have you ever, yourself, had experience or read in the literature, a case in which four children in the one family have all died from four different natural causes?'

'You mean suddenly, unexpectedly?' asked Professor Byard.

'Yes,' replied Mr Tedeschi.

'No, I don't.'

In his summing-up, the Crown prosecutor told the jury that lightning did not strike in the same place four times. 'Caleb may have died from a floppy larynx or SIDS. Patrick may have had an ALTE [acute life-threatening event] which was a first epileptic attack, an epileptic seizure. Sarah may have had a displaced uvula or SIDS. Laura may have had myocarditis . . . I can't disprove any of that.

'But one day some piglets might be born from a sow and the piglets might come out of the sow with wings on their backs and next morning Farmer Joe might look out of the kitchen window and see those piglets flying out of his farm. I can't disprove that either.

'Because if you look at what they [the defence] are suggesting, not in isolation but in totality, there has never, ever been before in the history of medicine – that our experts have been able to find – any case like this. It is preposterous. It is not a reasonable doubt. It is a fantasy.'

He instructed the jury to view the diaries as a machine to look into Kathleen Folbigg's mind and see what she was thinking and feeling. 'Imagine you had lost three of your children – what would you be writing? You would be writing about how cruel fate had been. About how unfair it was . . . The diaries contain ramblings about her weight, about her desire to be watched by men at discos, about her desperate desire to exercise to lose weight.'

He told the jury that the diary entries revealed Kathy's 'over-riding need to control, particularly the sleep and feeding patterns of the children' and how that had turned into a battle of wills that she 'was going to win'. In Sarah's case, he told the jury that if the baby 'hadn't battled so hard against the accused, the accused wouldn't have had to kill her'.

'With each child she was able to cope a little bit more, which is why each lived a little bit longer.'

Mr Tedeschi described Kathy's explanation of the diary entries during the taped police interview as 'glib, trite and evasive'.

The Crown prosecutor moved on to address any concerns the jury might have about Craig Folbigg lying to the police in his first statement. He told them that his actions could be explained because he was 'devoted, besotted by his wife; you might think somewhat dominated by his wife.

'For him to accept, to come to full realisation of her culpability, took a long time.'

Then the prosecutor highlighted ten things each of the deaths had in common including that they all happened suddenly, unexpectedly, at home, during a sleep period in a cot or bassinette and were discovered by the mother when she was the only person at home or awake. In four of the five incidents where Kathy found her children not breathing she did not render any assistance or even pick up the child. Three of the children were found dead by Kathy on a trip to the toilet. 'God, her going to the toilet was very dangerous for these children,' said Mr Tedeschi. 'God, you would be locking up the toilet, wouldn't you? Every one of them was during a normal check of their wellbeing. Gosh, you would be telling her not to check on them, wouldn't you? What an amazing coincidence. Or is it?' Finally he said it was another 'amazing coincidence' that the children had been found by their mother while they were still warm to the touch. Two still had a heartbeat.

They were not found cold and dead in bed in the morning as most SIDS victims were because their mother, deprived of sleep and overcome with stress, smothered them.

'Most probably she regretted what she had done – maybe that's why she raised the alarm.

'She did not pick them up because she had killed them.

'It might be difficult for you to emotionally get around the idea that a woman would murder her own children. It goes against any ounce of humanity,' said the Crown prosecutor. In conclusion, he summed up with the words: 'The only reasonable conclusion is that Kathleen Folbigg killed her children.'

It was a tough act to follow but Peter Zahra rose to the challenge. He told the jury that the Crown's ten points of coincidence evidence could be explained simply by the fact that Kathy was the primary caregiver. In fact, she was the one who showed enormous concern for the children and pushed for continued sleep studies to be carried out on Sarah. 'That is hard evidence that in the background of Sarah being unwell she was concerned enough to suggest that there be a further sleep study performed,' he said.

Mr Zahra told the jury that, contrary to the Crown's argument, Kathy had not murdered her children in a fit of frustration because she wanted to go to the gym and go out dancing. She had not even joined a gym until after the death of Sarah. 'Five or six months after the death of Sarah there was no going out,' said Mr Zahra. And no socialising on her own from the time Patrick died until after Laura was born.

'The Crown says she was prone to losing her cool. If this was the state of mind, if this was indicative of the accused being prone to lose control, why hasn't it manifested itself in a recognisable pattern of behaviour? There is no history of abuse, there is no suggestion that these children were abused by their mother.'

He urged the jury to go out to the jury room and listen again to the 000 tape of Kathy reporting that Laura was not breathing. 'You must ask the question:

is that the sound of a person who had just murdered her child?'

Peter Zahra told the jury that it should question the credibility of Craig Folbigg who had painted an increasingly sinister picture of his wife by unfavourably describing her attempts to regiment Laura's eating and sleeping patterns. 'These on their own are very minor things and they support the view that there has been an evolution in his evidence to make it more sinister towards the accused.

'It is submitted to you that there is really no evidence other than what Craig Folbigg says,' said Mr Zahra. 'You would have to look at Craig Folbigg's credibility generally.'

In conclusion, he cautioned the jury to look again at the diaries. 'Are they feelings of blame and guilt from murder or are they feelings of blame and guilt that she continued, after all these years, to ask the "what if" questions?'

It was time for Justice Graham Barr to sum up to the jury all the court had heard and guide them on the legal points. He warned them against speculating on why Kathy had not given evidence. 'The accused could have given evidence, but she has not and you may be wondering about that. Her silence is not evidence against her. You are not to treat it as an admission of guilt.'

He told the members of the jury to use their common sense and knowledge of human nature in coming to their verdicts. 'The facts of this case are likely to give rise to more emotion . . . it is unlikely to imagine a more tragic series of events happening to a single family. You must not judge this case with your hearts but with your heads.'

Justice Barr's summing-up of the trial ran over two days and finished on the morning of Wednesday 21 May. The prosecution had argued there was no room for a manslaughter verdict – Kathleen Folbigg was either guilty of murder or innocent. The judge outlined the legal issues to the jury and explained the difference between murder and manslaughter. Murder requires intent; manslaughter means there was no intent. Could Kathy have accidentally suffocated all four of her children?

It was now up to the jury to ponder the questions of guilt, innocence or just how many times lightning could strike in the same place.

The jury retired and the nail biting began.

17

Verdict

IT IS VERY COLD in the holding cells of the New South Wales Supreme Court at Darlinghurst. Kathy's bail had been revoked while the jury considered the verdict. She was sent downstairs from the dock to await the jury's verdict. Her heart thumped with dread. She had already spent six weeks in prison after Detective Bernie Ryan had arrested her in April 2001. Now here she was again. What would they decide? Would she be staring at walls like this for the rest of her life or would she be walking free again in a few hours? God, the suspense. It certainly gave her plenty of time to think. Her children. Her poor children. Craig's vicious tongue. Bernie Ryan. Funny, she didn't hate him; she had even smiled at him in court. He was just doing his job, like the media. Still, the defence had gone well. The jury would surely see that she was innocent. Her legs were shaking, juddering with the nerves. She couldn't stop them.

The cell door opened and in came Major Joyce Harmer again. The Salvation Army chaplain kept popping in to make sure she was all right, bringing her a few things to keep warm in the cold cell. Joyce understood that she did not feel like talking. What a good friend.

Kathy took stock. It was Wednesday 21 May 2003 and she was 35 years old, the mother of four dead babies and the estranged wife of a man who had completely assassinated her character in court. A man who had loved her since she was a teenager, but clearly no longer cared what happened to her. In another room upstairs, not far away, 12 complete strangers were deciding the course of the rest of her life. She wondered what was happening up there. What was taking them so long?

Twenty-five metres away, outside in the light of day, emotions were running high. Lea Bown was in tears. Quietly, she confided to reporters in the court that Craig was doing a deal with a media outlet to sell pictures of his four dead children. Her relationship with Craig was already strained. This did nothing to help. She was very upset at the prospect of Craig selling his children's images because she herself had lost a daughter to SIDS in 1974.

'You've all got a shock coming, I can tell you,' she told reporters in the court. Unbeknownst to anyone at the time, she had brokered a deal to give, free of charge, pictures of the children and Kathy as a child to one newspaper.

Craig's family was in a huddle on the top tier of the

foyer, keeping out of the way of the reporters milling around downstairs and the cameramen waiting outside on the steps of the courthouse. His sister Carol and brother Michael then ventured outside and called over a *Daily Telegraph* reporter. After a hurried conversation with them, the reporter returned to the media pack to announce the Folbiggs were looking for offers for their personal photographs of Caleb, Patrick, Sarah and Laura. Michael had told her that Craig should have a right to a percentage of the profits the media would make from this story. Although chequebook journalism is a part of modern life, many of the journalists were repulsed at the idea of the Folbiggs profiting from the sale of the photographs of the dead children. The idea was in direct contrast to the line Craig had maintained throughout the trial that he did not want his children to become a commodity.

Craig had carefully sequestered all the photographs of the children and had them under lock and key at his home in Singleton. He maintained it was to keep the memories of his children sacrosanct, but in the light of his brother's offer to the media, various media representatives now felt it was simply to push up the value of the photographs. At this point no one had seen a picture of any of the children. Even the videotape of Laura had been suppressed by the court.

Certainly the Folbiggs knew there was plenty of money that could be made. Only weeks earlier

Natasha Ryan, the Queensland schoolgirl who had hidden in her boyfriend's house for four years while her parents believed her to be dead, had been paid $250,000 to tell *Woman's Day* magazine and the '60 Minutes' television show her story.

That morning outside the court, representatives from '60 Minutes', 'Today Tonight' and 'A Current Affair' were making it clear to Craig Folbigg and his brother Michael that there was money on the table. They were up to $60,000 without even trying. After all, everyone was aware from the evidence in court that Craig mentioned, albeit jokingly at the time, that he would hire media fixer Harry M. Miller if it turned out his wife was a murderer. And a few people also knew about Kathy's conversation with Lea in which she had said that she wanted to sell her story and go on holiday to Queensland. It was a scramble for cash over four dead babies and no one was coming out of it in a good light.

Then Craig came down to put an end to it. He told the media pack that his brother had acted without his blessing. Michael had been looking out for him but that was not the way Craig wanted things done. He would make the photographs available to everyone.

Craig would change his mind a few more times about the availability of the photographs as the afternoon wore on. It did seem that he genuinely wanted to keep his children out of the media. In fact, he did not even have any photographs with him; they were all in Singleton. The only pictures at the court that day were colour photocopies taken for evidential reasons by Detective Ryan and Craig had not even known about these. Detective Ryan, however, who had already left the courthouse, would not release them without Craig's permission. Michael Folbigg, using a mobile phone, liaised between the two and the pictures finally arrived late in the day. It was dark by the time all the media outlets outside the court were able to make copies of the images of the photos. Michael Folbigg supervised the copying. 'Craig has given permission for these treasured photographs of his children to be released to put human faces to this tragedy. I want to dispel any rumours that Craig has received any payment or money for the photos. These are his beautiful children.'

Meanwhile, as all of these shenanigans occupied the minds of the people outside, the jury was considering its five verdicts. The day wore on and at ten to four in the afternoon everyone was called back in, as the judge had said they would be, to see if the jury wanted to carry on with its deliberations or return tomorrow. The consensus among the onlookers was that there might not be a verdict until Friday.

Kathy appeared in the dock and sat down. She looked pale and drawn. A frisson of excitement began among the Crown prosecutors at the lawyers' table and spread through the courtroom. The jury had reached a decision in less than six hours. There was going to be a verdict. Right now.

Justice Graham Barr called for silence and warned that anyone crying out would be ejected from the court. The jury filed in. The forewoman confirmed they had reached their verdicts. Kathy stood in the dock, eyes downcast. Tense. Major Harmer noticed Kathy trembling and worried that her legs would give way.

Inside the court the tension was palpable. No one present could ignore the lump in their throat or the knot in their stomach. The court official asked the jury forewoman what verdict had been reached on the first charge Kathleen Folbigg faced of murdering baby Caleb.

'Not guilty.' A collective gasp echoed though the court. Hands flew to mouths. Craig looked stunned.

The court official now asked for a verdict on the secondary charge of the manslaughter of Caleb.

'Guilty.' Another gasp erupted in the courtroom. It was different this time; it was more an expression of relief. Kathy's knees began to buckle but she managed to stay upright. She looked as though she had been hit.

Relentlessly the court official carried on, now asking for a verdict on the charge of grievous bodily harm against Patrick.

'Guilty.'

Murdering Patrick?

'Guilty.'

Murdering Sarah?

'Guilty.'

Murdering Laura?

'Guilty.'

Kathy was still on her feet, but hunched over, crying into her hands. The court official repeated back the verdicts.

'Guilty of the manslaughter of Caleb.

'Guilty of inflicting grievous bodily harm on Patrick.

'Guilty of the murder of Patrick.

'Guilty of the murder of Sarah.

'Guilty of the murder of Laura.'

The children's father, Craig, sitting at the back of the court, was struggling to contain his emotion. His sister Jen was crying. His stepmother Mary was in tears.

In the midst of all the emotion the judge thanked the jurors for the admirable way they had conducted themselves and excused them from jury duty for the next five years.

Kathy was still shaking, tears streaming down her red face. As she slumped into her seat, the jury filed out of court. A few jury members stole glances at her as they rose to leave the court for the last time. A weight had been lifted from their shoulders – it was now sitting where it belonged, on Kathy Folbigg.

Behind the dock, in the public gallery, Lea Bown wept. She did not believe Kathy was crying for her dead children out of remorse; she believed Kathy was really crying for herself out of self-pity. Around Lea, Craig's family were still in shock. Stunned. Their faces were all frozen in expressions of disbelief. Had it really happened? Had it come to this?

Kathy's sobs were now overwhelming. The Corrective Services officers were waiting to lead her away. She could not walk. With the judge's permission, Major Harmer rushed to her aid, putting her arm around Kathy and pushing a handkerchief into her hand.

'Okay Kathy, just come with me,' she said. Kathy's legs were shaking so badly that Major Harmer feared she would not be able to make it down the stairs. A Corrective Services officer took the major's bag as she led Kathy down.

It was now just after four o'clock. The prison van was waiting, ready to drive Kathy to Mulawa. Major Harmer wiped the tears from Kathy's eyes, who continued to sob uncontrollably, hugged the distraught woman goodbye, and turned to go. It was too much for Kathy; she could not bear seeing the Salvation Army chaplain walk away. Major Harmer pleaded with the officials and they let her go back into the cell. She hugged Kathy again. 'I will always be your friend,' she told the newly convicted murderer. The Corrective Services officers had to go. She walked the last few steps with Kathy to the prison van and said a final goodbye as the officers bundled her into the back of the van. Major Harmer watched the prison van drive away and then walked back up to the room where she had spent so much time with Kathy during the trial. Suddenly it hit her. Kathy was gone. She now shed a tear for her friend.

Outside the courthouse, Craig Folbigg stopped on the steps, shaken and upset. Reading from a brief prepared statement as the camera crews jostled around him with microphones and flashguns, he said: 'My most humble thanks go to 12 people I have never formally met who today share the honour of having set four beautiful souls free to rest in peace.' He thanked Detective Bernie Ryan for his dedication and 'dogged determination' and his fiancée for her support.

Craig was still reeling as he and his family headed to The Castle Hotel, a couple of blocks from the court-house, for a drink. It was not a celebration. There was no joy. Sad smiles. It was more of an ending. Four beautiful children were dead and someone they had loved was in jail. Craig had watched Kathy's head slump down in despair and felt badly for his wife of 16 years. He had loved her, possibly still did, and grieved for all that had been lost. Wasted. It had been extremely difficult for him to even countenance the thought that she may have been responsible for the deaths of their four children and now that he had reluctantly come to accept it, it was horrific to think that the person he had shared a significant part of his life with could have committed such crimes.

Later, Craig and one of his sisters joined Detective Ryan and the legal team at well-known Sydney lawyer's hotel The Crown. As the shock set in he spent much of the night in tears.

Lea Bown was still very upset too – torn between feeling terrible about her sister's fate and also acknowledging the evidence that Kathy had killed her own children. She decided to join everyone else for a drink rather than stay alone at her hotel and dwell on what had just happened to her estranged foster sister.

In a tribute to the closing speech of the trial, which indicated that if Kathleen Folbigg had not killed her children then pigs had just as much chance of flying, junior prosecutor Jane Culver presented Mark Tedeschi and Bernie Ryan with ceramic flying pigs to hang in their offices in recognition of their efforts. Detective Ryan was subdued and left early. It was the end of four hard years for him to see the woman he had always suspected of murdering her children convicted for what she did. He was triumphant, vindicated, but also sad that it had all come to this.

Mr Tedeschi knew exactly what it had taken Bernie Ryan to get to this point. 'He was an incredibly persistent investigator and without his remarkable dedication the matter would have never come to trial.

'In the initial parts of the investigation most of his colleagues set to dissuade him from putting much time or effort into the investigation because they felt it wouldn't go anywhere.

'He decided he didn't want to have a fifth child's death on his conscience and he pursued it relentlessly.

'His interview with Kathleen Folbigg was incredibly fair, unemotional and considerate towards her. He never had a vindictive attitude towards her and he was motivated by considerations of wanting to see justice done.'

As everybody at the pub reflected on the lives and deaths of four little children and the years of heartache that had led to the verdict, the woman who had been responsible for causing it all was curled up in a foetal position in a high-security cell at Mulawa Women's Prison. She had barely stopped sobbing since she had left court. The death threats from other prisoners were already starting. You might be a hero in jail for killing your husband but murder your kids and you were target number-one, the most hated woman inside. Already she was isolated for her own protection. What madness had brought her to this point?

Detective Ryan had pondered Kathleen Folbigg's state of mind for a long time. His conclusion left no room for doubt. 'She wasn't mad, just bad.'

At the time the verdict had been delivered, Kathy's former lover Tony Lambkin was working on a building site in the Hunter Valley countryside. Following his usual routine, he went to The Agricultural Hotel in Singleton for a drink with his brother Bart and a coterie of old friends.

By the time he reached the hotel he had been tipped off by *Sun-Herald* journalist Eamonn Duff that the verdict was due. When he walked into the bar the television in the corner was switched to Channel Nine. The journalist was waiting for him and pushed a beer into his hand.

Kathy was the lead item on the news. As her face flashed up on the screen the entire pub fell silent. Every eye in the place moved from the screen to Tony's face and back again. Everyone knew what she meant to him. As the news was reported on how clear cut the verdict had been in proclaiming Kathy guilty for the murder of her children, tears streamed down Tony's face. His mates felt awkward. They wanted to comfort him but were not really sure how to react.

The atmosphere in the old-style pub remained uncomfortable and subdued after the news had finished. Tony Lambkin did what many people would have done under the same circumstances – he got drunk.

And if that was not enough, the following night he stood at the bar again while a television station ran footage from the police interview with Kathy denying she had killed her children. Once again the bar fell silent as the barman turned up the volume. Tony Lambkin relived the ordeal. The agony for him was that all of his friends in the bar had met Kathy through him and had previously taken his explanation of her innocence at face value. In fact, they had all liked Kathy. However, now his friends had had time to think about Kathy's trial. Tony was still protesting her innocence, thinking with his heart, while his friends were finding it hard to dismiss the facts. Up until the previous night they had been completely unaware that Kathy's father had killed her mother and many had not read the diary entries in the papers. Now, many of them felt Kathy had betrayed both Tony and themselves. There was an enormous sense of sympathy in the pub that night along with the feeling that, perhaps, their friend had lost his heart to the wrong lady.

18

Sentence

IT COULD ALL HAVE ended so very differently. In England, less than a month later a mother the same age as Kathleen Folbigg walked free from an almost identical trial. Pharmacist Trupti Patel, 35, had been charged with deliberately suffocating 22-day-old Amar Patel in 1997, 15-day-old Jamie Patel in 1999 and 13-and-a-half week old Mia Patel in 2001. When the jury returned its not-guilty verdicts Mrs Patel's family and friends erupted in a gigantic cry of 'Yes!' from the public gallery. She came out of the dock to embrace her loyal husband and was reunited with her surviving eight-year-old daughter. Her solicitor, Margaret Taylor, said to the media: 'Few mothers will ever have to experience the death of one baby, let alone the death of three. Virtually no mother, however, will subsequently face the trauma of being accused of deliberately suffocating her children. The jury have today concluded that she played no part in the tragic death of Amar, Jamie and Mia. She walks from the court as a free woman.'

Two women who suffered the loss of their children. Two very different outcomes. While Trupti Patel returned to her everyday life, Kathleen Folbigg was in prison, planning her appeal. She had always maintained that she was innocent. The jury in her case did not agree.

Kathy had been receiving death threats. Whenever she walked out of her high-security cell, guards would walk on either side of her to protect her from attacks from other prisoners from the front and sides while another walked behind to stop attacks coming from the rear. She was invited to have input in this book. She at first agreed and then declined. In her first letter she admitted that she was facing life as '*the most hated woman around at the moment*'. She was hurting badly and undecided if she should try to get her side of what really happened into the public eye. She was worried that Craig had done too much damage. She wrote:

I have already suffered greatly at the hands of Craig and his capability to deliver with his tongue. And his quite amazing ability to turn simple into exaggerated and extravagant tales. I do not and will not permit myself to be attacked such as that again.

It was also very hard for her to trust again:

I am non-trusting, suspicious, wary and protective beyond all in regards to my life. Already I have been misquoted, my diaries misunderstood and inferred incorrectly, my personality and demeanour savagely attacked thus my character assumed to be anything other than what I really am. I am not stupid. To allow any encroachment I believe would merely be means to attempt more of the same.

I am coping, just. As for my stress and strains of the past few weeks – that is an understatement. My stress has been for years, not weeks, and it was just a culmination of all that occurred recently. Much more is yet to come. I now face being the most 'hated' woman around at the moment and death threats are a real consideration. Loneliness, devastating heartache about all that has happened, delayed grief for my children, especially Laura, and much more. In this regard observations made about my 'stoic, cool, un-emotional' demeanour were correct. It's the only way to survive such an attack on one's soul. Also 'they' fail to see one important factor – I didn't have the choice to be any other way. I would not of been useful in own defence. I succumbed once to my feelings during the trial and proved to myself that becoming devastated by all, could not help me now. The day may come where it is time to release all, but till my battle is done in clearing my name and reputation, that day is not yet.

She was upset because she mistakenly believed that Craig and his family were receiving financial rewards 'at the *expense of my life and memories of my children*'. And in her second letter posted the very next day she decided that she could not speak out because at that stage:

> *My appeal process has yet to be finalised. I still do not agree with my memories and life and my children's lives being exploited in this manner. I am a private person and will remain so. My distrust is too deep.*

In jail Kathy received a devastating letter from Lea Bown, the sister who provided the police with a series of tapes of telephone conversations they had shared. Kathy's barrister Peter Zahra, SC, had observed during the trial that Department of Community Services reports into her foster family indicated there were underlying tensions in the family. The relationship between Kathy and Lea had always been particularly difficult, despite periods where their relationship seemed amicable. In part the letter told Kathy that Lea hoped she could get the help she so badly needed because it was the only way she would ever be able to find peace and 'come to terms with things'.

Kathy replied to this letter and her sister handed the letter straight over to the *Daily Telegraph* in Sydney, which used it again on the front page under the headline 'I'm the most HATED woman alive'. Lea told the paper that she no longer felt the need to protect or stand up for Kathy because she now saw her for what she was – a monster and murderer.

In the letter to her sister Kathy had written:

Dear Lea,

What do you say to people who refuse to hear? You are amongst that group. Such a shame. Lea – I will not answer you in regard to what you think I have done. I'm tired of saying the same thing again and again, only to be ignored and have everyone else tell me I'm a liar.

Lea – you chose to betray me. You chose to believe Craig and [the] police.

You chose to only see the worst and take it as fact.

You chose to pull back and sacrifice me.

You chose your inability to think for yourself over me.

Lea – you chose – I didn't.

Yes, you're correct. I am not my father. I questioned myself about that once. But I have always fought my father's connection.

Deirdre and Neville Marlborough were my parents, my influences, traits, gifts, etc are from them. Are they capable of such things? Are you? No, so why am I, Lea?

Why would I do anything that makes me even remotely like such a man.

Lea – I hold no grudges or hatred or anything else

anymore. I've been through too much to bother with such negative emotions.

You surprised me greatly. Lea – you purposely lied, deceived, manipulated me. Only comment about my diaries is exactly that. They're mine, not yours, not anyone's . . . mine, what I was feeling and what I wrote, and all I'll say is everyone has no right to be so presumptuous as to know what I meant or was saying.

They are not literal, definitely not a window to my brain – how ridiculous. They were a place for me to offload and then wipe my hands and move on.

There's a huge difference from inferring murder to doing it. But I will not explain to narrow-minded people who refuse to even try to think about it.

Everyone forgets how this situation started, Craig's . . . vengeance for leaving him.

Has it ever occurred to you that of all my diaries, 1996–98 were the only ones kept.

They were the darkest years of my life. I did nothing but overanalyse and self criticise and just tear myself apart. I did not ask questions, but they were so critical and deep, I doubt anyone could possibly understand. You like so many others certainly didn't.

But enough, I know you're not believing any of it. And it doesn't matter. You have convinced yourself you're right and just nothing I say will make a difference.

Lea – I know my failures and have taken full responsibility for them, but I will not be forced to take responsibility for something I have not done. I have no more energy to battle with people who won't hear.

Lea – try to imagine your life being spread out, ripped to pieces, examined, opinions cast, character assassinated, your every word, action, thought, doubted, and you're told you don't know yourself.

Add to that, because of all of the above, becoming the most HATED *woman alive.*

You can't. I now live with that every day. I'm strong enough, you're obviously not. I endure all of this knowing that vindication will one day be mine.

I cry every night at the thought that there are people out there that think I'm capable of such things. I cry because I discovered my own sister thought that.

Well, I won't comment further on such terrible thought of me. Lea, I don't like being hated so why would I do something that ensures I am? That is the last time I'll state – I did not kill my children.

Oh, I know you're thinking I'm in denial etc, etc. I'm not. I know what the truth is. I can't help it if so many others can't.

Lea – for 12 months Craig did the same . . . all in an attempt to get me to confess.

But it never happened, because I have nothing to confess.

Lea – it took four years to come up with a totally

circumstantial, non-factual, hearsay case.

It's a sad day when a mother can be put away for merely being a normal mother, who wrote down her emotions, anxieties and frustrations in bloody books.

You know, as well as I do, I'm not capable of such disgusting acts of violence.

I am fine, if you care. Press were wrong, as usual. Obviously, you still haven't learnt that they never tell the truth. I never have been in danger, was never moved from where I am.

Lea, I love my family, I always have. I am not ashamed of myself or feel I have shamed any of you.

Oh, it doesn't matter, I know you didn't want to believe me, it would mean you'd have to concede that you were wrong and I know you Lea, you will never do that.

Say hello to the rest of the family. If you wish to.

Regrettably,
Your sister,
Kathy.

On Friday 29 August 2003 Kathleen Folbigg again travelled to the Supreme Court for her lawyers to make submissions on her sentence. Gathered were the same cast of family, friends, lawyers, media and onlookers who had last seen her led from the dock in tears three months previously. Craig did not attend the sentencing hearing. He had been expected to stand up and give a victim impact statement. In the end he decided against it. His brother Michael's wife attended with his stepmother and said Craig was dealing with a lot of issues. Avoiding the media glare and resultant publicity was one way of coping. Michael said Craig was trying to get on with his life with his new partner. Perhaps one day they would have children – even though Craig knew that this would rekindle the media interest in his life. According to Michael, Craig did not need to attend the court because he did not expect to find out why his wife killed their children.

'Craig has got his peace. He knows how his children died and he is resigned to the fact he may never know why. At the end of the day we really don't know the answers. Kathy needs to say "Yes I did this", but at the moment she is maintaining her innocence,' said Michael.

The three months since Kathy's last appearance before Justice Graham Barr had not been kind to her. She entered the dock looking tired and wan with a corrective services officer at her shoulder. She had put on weight and the black smudges from lack of sleep were starkly outlined beneath her eyes. Her hair, so perfectly groomed during the trial, looked barely brushed and now had dark grey and brown patches growing through the red dye. She was wearing the same blue jacket, burgundy pants, cheap high-heeled shoes and, most tellingly of all about her state of mind, no make-up. Her skin was pallid. Being the most hated woman inside the most violent prison in New South Wales was clearly taking its toll. She flicked a quick glance around the court, took in the reassuringly friendly presence of Major Joyce Harmer, and then angled her body away from the journalists sitting next to her in the media box of the bright modern court-room. She studied a neutral piece of carpet. A burgundy handkerchief remained clenched tightly in her hands. Her face betrayed no emotion.

Kathy did not acknowledge her sister, Lea Bown, who watched intently from the packed public gallery. Also in court, with his wife Kel by his side, was newly promoted Detective Inspector Bernie Ryan. Now based in Goulburn, he had become something of a national expert on child murders. He had become the first point of contact for many police forces who, as a result of Ryan's work on the Folbigg case, were looking into occurrences of multiple child deaths within individual families.

Before the submissions began, Kathy's legal-aid barr-ister Peter Zahra SC had been anxious. Once in the court, appearing before Justice Graham Barr, he again put his heart and soul into the fight for the best possible outcome for his client. He called forensic psychiatrist Dr Bruce Westmore to the stand. This was the moment many in the court had waited for – could there be an explanation for what had so far been an inexplicable crime?

Psychiatrists had already been scratching their heads in bemusement about the possible causes of Kathleen Folbigg's crimes. Forensic psychiatrist Dr Rod Milton had concluded: 'I am sure we will never know why she did it. I think we will get 20 answers but I wouldn't care to say how many of those are correct. The current state of psychology and psychiatry is not equal to explaining such a thing – but it will try.' Australian and New Zealand College of Psychiatrists New South Wales branch chairwoman Louise Newman felt the answer may never be forthcoming from Kathy herself because of dissociation. In forensic psychiatry this is the term used for people who block out their memory of traumatic events; people might be so overwhelmed by anxiety that they forget or repress the traumatic event that has happened. Louise Newman was also reported as saying that there was some research that people who abuse children may also forget what they have done or only have hazy memories of carrying out the abuse. Abusers can interpret these recollections very differently but it is not a conscious interpretation.' 'The interesting question is whether, in general, someone who has committed serious offences can actually believe themselves to be innocent.'

In court Dr Westmore said Folbigg was not psychotic but was suffering from a deep-seated personality disorder. It could not be classified. It simply did not fit into any of the 14 clinically defined personality disorders so fell into a final category of unclassifiable disorders. The origins of the disorder stemmed from her mistreatment as a child up to the age of three before she was put into foster care. Because such an early part of her life was traumatic, the pessimistic prognosis was that the disorder was untreatable. The psychiatric reports showed that as a baby Kathy had suffered physical, emotional and possibly sexual abuse. Her mother had regular dumped her with an aunt and uncle and, as a result, Kathy did not receive consistent care from her parents. After her father killed her mother when she was 18 months old Kathy was placed with the aunt and uncle and began to act out in a manner that suggested she had suffered sexual abuse. Her behaviour and development became so bad that it was feared she was retarded. It was only once she was placed with the Marlboroughs that she began to blossom and develop into what her foster mother Deirdre called a 'sweet and helpful' little girl. Her annual Department of Community Services reports and school reports revealed a normal and healthy child who appeared to be dedicated and work hard. There were a few behavioural problems in her teens that were attributed to the large age gap between Kathy and her foster mother. She clashed with her foster parents as a 15-year-old but calmed down again and was able to bond perfectly normally three years later with her boyfriend Craig. For Dr Westmore this was something he simply did not understand. She appeared to have perfectly normal relations from the age of three onwards until she killed her first child when she was 21. Her crimes were an enigma. From her diaries he said it was clear that she suffered severe depression and feelings of abandonment, isolation, inadequacy and vulnerability. Kathy herself acknowledged this in one diary entry and said she coped with it by eating chocolate and junk food. Dr Westmore referred to the long-held psychiatric belief that depression was internalised rage. Over time, particularly after arguments with Craig, he said Kathy may have taken out that anger on her children. Her depression and personality problems put in place a mechanism within her that could not cope with her children once they began to express their own wills. It meant she could not be trusted with any future children of her own or with the lives of any put into her care.

Crown prosecutor Mark Tedeschi QC spoke next. He said the diaries showed Kathy was aware of the danger she presented to her children. Instead of protecting them, she put her own life, marriage and good name first. As a result, the children died. But they did not go without a fight. Each baby struggled for up to four minutes before finally suffocated. 'These were not peaceful deaths,' said Mr Tedeschi. He asked Justice Graham Barr to impose a life sentence. He said the crime was far worse than that of Craig Merritt, who killed his three children in one alcohol-fuelled moment and then pleaded guilty before receiving a life sentence. By contrast, Kathy had carried out four homicides over 10 years and still maintained her innocence.

Mr Zahra told the judge that a life term did not have to mean natural life. Instead, he asked for a determinate sentence, possibly one that would take into account Kathy's childbearing years to accommodate Dr Westmore's belief that she could not be trusted with her own or anyone else's child in her sole care. Dr Westmore said Kathy needed regular psychiatric consultations but would not receive them in prison. She would be isolated in her cell for her own protection for 22 hours a day. The other two hours outside her cell would also be spent alone. 'It is essentially an experience of isolation,' Dr Westmore said. 'It will lead to a numbing of her social expressions, loss of social skills, isolation, depression and paranoia.'

At the end of the hearing, Justice Graham Barr announced that he would take time to consider his sentence and would let all parties know when he was ready to return it. Kathy stood as he left the court and then, looking pale and drawn from the ordeal, was escorted back to the loneliness of her cell. More waiting.

The view of Kathy's isolated life ahead was confirmed after the hearing by the commander of women's prisons in New South Wales, Lee Downes. '[Kathy] is not a person we would take a chance with. The nature of the offence means she would be forever separate. Her social contact is with staff, uniformed and non-uniformed, and I guess she will always be housed separately. We will assess if she can have limited contact with other women down the track, but it is a day-by-day, month-by-month case with anybody who has been so public, who has allegedly committed a crime other inmates take a set against,' she said. This meant that Kathy was to be checked every half-hour as part of a suicide watch and was never to have a prison job for fear of attack. The only time that she would be able to move from the 40-prisoner isolation wing was to be when every other prisoner was under lock and key.

Alongside Kathy in Mulawa prison was Belinda van Krevel, who had conspired to murder her own father, and Katherine Knight, who had skinned her husband and cooked his head in a pot. Unlike Kathy, fellow Hunter-Valley killer Katherine Knight was doing well. In jail you are a hero if you kill your partner but a pariah if you kill your children. Ms Downes, who has been governor of Mulawa, Emu Plains, Grafton and Parklea prisons, said: 'Prisoners have different reactions; some hit the law books and study for their appeal, some say what's the point. Sometimes people go a bit mad. They get mental illness as a result of going to jail, or it worsens the mental illness they had. If someone sat around in the same place for 20, 30, 40 years they would go brain dead.' She said the majority of the 500 women incarcerated in New South Wales are victims of sexual assault, incest, domestic violence or have witnessed physical abuse. 'As adults, they get the same thing again and when they come into jail: we have a whole range of security procedures which unfortunately bring back these experiences.' She felt that Kathy would inevitably become institutionalised.

Outside prison, Kathy's husband Craig was still dealing with trauma himself. As the wait for the sentencing dragged on Craig suffered. 'He is up and down like a pair of stripper's knickers,' said his brother Michael. He believed his brother needed the closure the sentence would bring and that it would also release Craig from the fear he felt. 'I know of some stuff that happened between the two of them in the past; I mean, she has a very violent temper and will just lash out without warning. I think he is in mortal fear of her. He needs to know she has gone away and cannot come back to harm him – or his future children, for that matter.' But despite the emotional upheaval, Michael said his brother also spent much of the time planning for his future and for his marriage to Helen Pearce.

The day had finally come. On Friday 24 October 2003 Kathleen Folbigg once again sat in the dock for what her family and friends hoped would be the final act in the tragedy of her four children's deaths. Justice Graham Barr had now considered the submissions he received at the sentencing hearing on 29 August 2003, and was ready to hand down Kathleen's sentence. It was to prove a day of yet more astonishing emotional bombshells.

Kathy looked pale and drawn, having now spent more than five months behind bars in Mulawa Women's Prison since her trial. She angled her body away from the packed public gallery, as she had done during the sentencing hearing, and focused intently on the bench from where Justice Graham Barr would deliver the sentence. She was wearing the same blue jacket from the earlier trial but, unlike her previous court appearances, she had made no attempt to coordinate it with any of her other clothes. If it was the case that one could determine Kathy's mood by the state of her hair, as her foster sister, Lea Bown, had claimed, then Kathy was in despair. Her hair appeared unbrushed and was pulled back from her face with a tight band. Life in prison – kept in isolation and flanked by prison guards for her own protection during the two hours she was allowed out of her cell every day – was clearly not an easy ride.

Craig waited until the representatives of every media organisation in Sydney had settled into their seats before he slipped into the back row of the wood-panelled room of the Supreme Court. His sister Patricia Newitt and brothers Michael and John accompanied him. Lea Bown sat in the front row with her husband, Ted, and a support group of friends. Detective Inspector Bernie Ryan grinned from the gallery at people he knew. Both legal teams nodded to familiar faces as they waited for the knock that heralded Justice Barr's arrival in the crowded court.

Justice Barr delivered his words in a calm, measured tone, stopping regularly for drinks of water or to repeat a phrase that had been drowned out by coughing from the public gallery. He began with a brief history of Kathleen's life with Craig and the birth of their first baby, Caleb. With economical thoroughness, he ran through the evidence surrounding the death of each of the four children. And then he attempted to do what everyone had wondered and wanted from the outset of the trial. He began to suggest a reason why Kathleen Folbigg had killed her children.

'It is necessary to try to understand why the offender lost her temper and assaulted her children,' he said. He explained that in an attempt to understand her state of mind he would draw on records from the government department that had been responsible for overseeing Kathleen in her youth, as well as her own personal diaries and the opinion of psychiatrists on that material.

It was particularly the government documents from over 30 years before that provided explosive revelations and offered significant insight into the behaviour of Kathleen Folbigg.

After Kathleen's father had murdered her mother she was made a ward of the state and placed in the care of her mother's sister, Mrs Platt. A departmental report on 21 May 1970 showed that Mrs Platt had reported she was having trouble teaching young Kathy the basic requirements of hygiene and acceptable behaviour. Kathy was aggressive towards other children, prone to severe temper tantrums and preoccupied with her sexual organs. She had been seen trying to insert various objects into her vagina. She was quickly referred to the Yagoona Child Health Clinic where she was assessed by Dr Spencer. In a report on 12 June 1970, two days before Kathy's third birthday, he noted Mrs Platt's complaints that Kathy was indulging in excessive sex play and masturbation. He concluded that Kathy had been sexually misused by her father during infancy. Some 33 years after this report was filed, there were audible gasps in the courtroom at this horrific revelation. Only Kathy remained unmoved, legs crossed, her gaze focused solely on the red-gowned judge who continued to recount the details of her deeply troubled childhood.

Kathy had been withdrawn from the Platts in July 1970 when she was three years old and sent to Bidura Children's Home. Psychologists assessed her and found her to be of borderline retarded intelligence – remote, restless, inattentive and unresponsive when shown individual attention. She rarely smiled but over the following month became more approachable and interested in her surroundings and other people.

In September 1970 she was placed into the foster care of Mr and Mrs Marlborough and began to overcome her difficult start to life. For the most part, other than some moodiness, she seemed a likeable, friendly and intelligent child, and showed considerable affection for the Marlboroughs, who wanted to adopt her.

There were some periods of difficulty as a teenager. Things were not always easy for her in high school and she was discharged on two stealing charges. But otherwise she had appeared to overcome her early years of trauma.

In 1984, however, she suffered a severe setback when she was told her father had murdered her mother. The teenager made contact with the Platts who gave her some photographs of herself as a baby, and also of her mother. But she did not pursue a relationship with them. During this time her relationship with the Marlboroughs became strained until it finally broke down when she was seventeen. Not long after this, she began her relationship with Craig Folbigg.

Justice Barr said he accepted the evidence of psychiatrists who had visited Kathy in jail that by the time she was 18 months old she was a seriously disturbed and regressed little girl. 'It is well established that children who are neglected and suffer serious physical and sexual trauma may suffer a profound disturbance of personality development. The evidence for such a disturbance in the offender is strong, as her diaries reveal,' the judge said. He then proceeded to read from several passages of Kathleen's diaries.

The diaries, written by Kathy solely for herself, painted a picture of a very lonely and depressed woman. During her trial she had not given evidence. Now, Kathleen was finally given a voice through the diary entries that Justice Barr read out as part of his judgment to demonstrate her state of mind.

On 16 July 1996, nearly three years after Sarah's death, and one year before Laura was born, she had written:

Sometimes I feel life is a film scene, just practised and rehearsed, each actor perfect and surreal, times I don't fit in the play, have never fit, but keep attempting to anyway for fear of being isolated and alone. Times – I feel alone anyway no matter who I'm with.

Three weeks later, on 9 August 1996, Kathy had recognised her feelings of depression and alienation and recorded in her diary:

Been feeling weird lately – depressed, indecisive, etc. Not my usual self. Can't seem to put my finger on what's wrong . . . Feeling lonely! I know that's silly because I have friends I can see but I suppose it's because I want friends that will come to see me and want to be with me. I usually feel that I'm intruding or pushing my way onto people. Okay, enough self analysing. It's my ego and weight problem that's giving me a bashing. Rang to go back to JIC – they haven't bothered to return my call. Feeling left out, taken for granted, unattractive and self centred. There, I've purged myself. Now to change all this, is up to me – as usual.

It was during this time that she trying to become pregnant with her fourth child. A month later, on 11 September 1996, she confided:

Feeling inferior doesn't help. Feeling inadequate because I'm not pregnant yet. Feel as though it's my fault. Think it's deserved. After everything that's happened.

I suppose I deserve to never have kids again. I am just so depressed. Don't know what to do. Feel like taking the rest of the week off. But know my pay will be grossly affected if I do.

Around the time Kathy became pregnant, she was still feeling very depressed and lonely. Her diary entry on 13 November 1996 revealed her feelings:

Not sure why I'm so depressed lately. Seem to be suffering mood swings. I also have no energy lately either . . . Why is family so important to me? I now have the start of my very own, but it doesn't seem good enough. I know Craig doesn't understand. He has the knowledge of stability and love from siblings and parents even if he chooses to ignore them. Me – I have no one but him. It seems to affect me so – why should it matter? It shouldn't.

These feelings of low self-esteem were just as evident in the New Year. On 14 January 1997 she wrote:

Not happy with myself lately. Finally starting to physically show that I'm pregnant. Doesn't do much for the self esteem. Don't get me wrong. I couldn't be happier – it's just Craig's roving eye will always be of concern to me. I suppose this is a concept known by all women. We are vulnerable emotionally at this stage. So everything is exaggerated tenfold.

Kathy recognised some of the triggers of her stress, as described in her diary on 17 February 1997:

> Found [Craig's] jealous already of bub. He says he only has six months left to be with me and for me. Hopefully I've explained that's not true – he should be for me, forever, just because a baby is entering our life makes no difference really. One day it will leave. The others did, but this one's not going in the same fashion. This time I'm prepared and know what signals to watch out for in myself. Changes in mood etc. Help I will get if need be. I also know that my lethargy and tiredness and continued rejection of him had a bad effect.

Her fears about the stability of her marriage seemed to become even more exacerbated as her pregnancy wore on. On 30 May 1997 she wrote:

> Got myself in quite an emotional state last night . . . Felt, feeling very alone, unattractive and now uncomfortable with the many thoughts that are running through my mind about the stability of our relationship. This is not the time to be upset and stressing over everything. He pulls away from me if I touch him in any other way than comforting. Feel as though I've lost him, that his feelings for me aren't the same any more. Never felt so alone in all my life.

In the seventh month of her pregnancy, Kathy referred in a diary entry dated 6 June 1997 to her moods and also to her future baby's survival:

From now on though I'm sure [Craig's] attention and focus will change from me to his child and so it should. I couldn't see that before. I was very selfish when it came to Craig's attention. Hopefully this time we have both learned how to share it but still manage to keep a little something aside for just each other. We will see . . . maybe then he will see when stress of it all is getting to be too much and save me from ever feeling like I did before, during my dark moods. Hopefully preparing myself will mean the end of my dark moods, or at least the ability to see it coming and say to him or someone, hey, help I'm getting overwhelmed here, help me out. That will be the key to this baby's survival. It surely will.

On 11 June 1997 Kathy revealed more feelings to her diary, reflecting her sense of worthlessness and an expectation of the mix of emotions the immediate future would bring:

If it wasn't for my baby coming soon, I'd sit and wonder again what I was put on this earth for, what contribution have I made to anyone's life? Only person I think I've made a difference to is Craig. And at times like this, I can't do anything for him so I fail there as well. 30 years, first five I don't really remember, rest I don't choose to remember, last 10–11 have been filled with trauma, tragedy, happiness, mixed emotions of all desires. Maybe from now on I'll be able to settle a little. But no. Immediate future brings turmoil happiness, sad memories, happy ones, depression, great pride and it goes on . . . life sux. You can never figure it out – is anyone meant to?

Laura was born in August. Six weeks later, in a diary entry written on 20 September 1997, Kathy's feelings of resentment towards Craig, in the wake of the birth of their child, were evident:

I can't even trust or depend on him to look after her properly. He refuses to bother to learn anything about her. He doesn't pay attention when feeding her, hasn't changed a nappy, doesn't do washing or ironing, only washes up once in a while. His life continues as normal. Work, come home and I look after him. He doesn't even cook tea every now and then unless I ask him to. And then it is begrudgingly. What do I do? The only break I get is when I go to aerobics three half hours a week. But these are times is not enough. I know, my feelings are normal – I'm just venting. But at the moment I, [indecipherable] wish I hadn't made the decision to have her, but then all I have to do is look at her and all that melts away. Well, I just pissed Craig off, he's up and out of bed now. Complaining he can't sleep.

Six months later, Kathy was still expressing the same sentiments about Craig and her frustration with

looking after Laura all of the time, as her diary entry
of 13 March 1998 shows:

> *Feeling very dissatisfied tonight. With myself, my life,*
> *Craig. What can I do . . . I need him to take some of the*
> *stress of looking after her off me. He seems to be failing*
> *lately.*

After Kathleen Folbigg's trial she was visited five times
by a forensic psychiatrist named Dr Michael Giuffrida. Justice Barr drew heavily on his reports to
conclude in his judgment that Kathleen did not suffer
a conduct disorder or an antisocial personality disorder stemming from her difficult childhood. Unlike
most mothers who kill their children, Kathleen
Folbigg was not psychotic, in Dr Giuffrida's opinion.
She dealt with the psychiatrist as if she was not
responsible for the deaths of her children. He thought
her diary entries were the writings of a greatly tor-
mented and exceedingly disturbed woman. The psychiatrist noted the prevailing theme of intensely
depressed mood, expressions of worthlessness and low
self-esteem, as well as the references to feelings of
rejection and abandonment by her husband, family
and friends. Those irreversible feelings were the result
of the experiences she endured as a little girl.

Dr Giuffrida said that Kathleen had approached
childbirth with intense anxiety and was fearful that

the task of mothering was beyond her. The psychiatrist's report attempted to explain how Kathleen Folbigg's persistent state of depression contributed strongly to her killing her children. During the interviews he found her to be of at least average intelligence and with 'remarkably little' to implicate any of the serious personality disorders commonly found in women who kill their children. He noted that her reaction to the death of each of her children was characterised by almost an absence of normal grief and bereavement. There was no profound and long-lasting grieving process nor the symptoms of post-traumatic stress disorder he would have expected from her after smothering the children. The reason for this emotional detachment was that in her first 18 months of life she was highly likely to have been raised in a dysfunctional environment, suffering emotional, physical and possibly sexual abuse by her father. She was also neglected by her mother.

Dr Giuffrida found it highly significant that tests conducted on her in 1970 found her to be regressed and suffering behavioural difficulties when it was clear later that she was of average or above average intelligence. He was of the opinion that Kathy's regression suggested she had been severely traumatised in the first 18 months of life. Three-year-old Kathy's preoccupation with her genitals and the fact she was inserting objects into her vagina was prima facie evidence that she had been sexually abused. For the most part, evidence in medical literature indicates that children who endure serious sexual and physical trauma and neglect suffer a profound disturbance of personality development. In Kathleen Folbigg's case this meant she had suffered possibly irreversible impairment of her capacity to develop any meaningful emotional bonding or attachment, which in turn meant she could not care for and protect her own children.

Justice Barr also drew on the evidence and the psychiatric report of Dr Westmore, which suggested Kathleen's depression manifested as anger. Her diaries had become an outlet for her to express her internal feelings of rage, frustration and perhaps homicidal impulses and thoughts. It was possible to say from the diary entries that there was a relationship between the depression and the feelings of anger that led to the deaths of the children.

The judge took another sip of water and shot a glance across the court to where Kathleen Folbigg sat, unresponsive to everything she had heard so far. There were, he said, several factors in the case that made it liable to be viewed more seriously and as attracting a higher penalty. The five attacks took place on four children over a period of 10 years. The victims all depended on the offender, their mother, for their nurture and survival. She had broken their trust. But

Justice Barr dismissed the prosecution's claims that in having more children she had put her own desires ahead of their needs. He said Kathleen believed she would be able to overcome the danger she presented to each child. He concluded that the attack on Caleb, like those on the other children, resulted from her uncontrollable anger. With the second fatal attack on Patrick, Justice Barr said he was satisfied that in her anger Kathleen Folbigg had decided to rid herself of the child whose presence she could no longer tolerate. And there was no room for doubt that when she killed Sarah and Laura she intended to do so. The judge felt, however, that Kathleen was psychologically damaged and barely coping in her day-to-day life. The attacks on her children were not premeditated but happened when she was pushed beyond her capacity to manage. Afterwards, she falsely pretended the unexpected discovery of an accident and maintained her innocence because she could not admit her failure to anyone but herself. Her anger cooled as fast as it had arisen and her attempts to get medical help for her children were genuine. The judge concluded that Kathleen Folbigg was not a cruel mother. She did not systematically abuse her children; they were well clothed and fed and regularly attended to by doctors for standard medical check-ups. But the abuse she had suffered as a baby had left her unable to form any normal, loving rela-tionships. She was unable to confide in her husband,

Craig, and he left her to cope because he did not realise she was at the end of her tether.

The future that Justice Barr painted for Kathleen Folbigg was bleak. She would always be a danger if given the responsibility of caring for a child. 'That must never happen,' he said. Her condition was largely untreatable. The depression might respond to medication and the feelings of failure could respond to psychotherapy, although it was unlikely to be available fortnightly in jail, as Dr Westmore had recommended she needed. She was unlikely to ever admit her offences to anyone other than herself. If she did so it would make her a high suicide risk. 'Such an end will always be a risk in any event,' the judge said.

Justice Barr acknowledged that jail was a particularly dangerous place for Kathy because of the risk of being harmed or murdered by other inmates and said that her regime of being kept in isolation and locked up for 22 out of every 24 hours was likely to continue indefinitely, thus making the serving of her sentence all the more difficult for her. However, Justice Barr spoke of the need for the sentence to reflect the outrage of the community and to deter other people from committing similar crimes – crimes so difficult to detect.

At last the moment had arrived. Kathleen was on her feet, awaiting Justice Barr's sentencing. It felt as though everyone in the public gallery had taken a collective breath and held it. As if to prove everything the psychiatrists had said about her emotional detachment, Kathleen remained composed and calm. There was going to be no hysterical collapse this time. The court was completely silent and still. The tension was palpable. In his considered tone, Justice Barr began to deliver the sentence that members of Kathleen's and Craig's families had waited so long to hear.

'Kathleen Megan Folbigg, for the manslaughter of Caleb Gibson Folbigg I sentence you to imprisonment for 10 years. The sentence will be taken to have commenced on 22 April 2003 and will expire on 21 April 2013. I decline to fix a non-parole period,' said the judge.

'For the intentional infliction of grievous bodily harm upon Patrick Allen Folbigg I sentence you to imprisonment for 14 years. The sentence will commence on 22 April 2005 and will expire on 21 April 2019. I decline to fix a non-parole period.

'For the murder of Patrick Allen Folbigg I sentence you to imprisonment for 18 years. The sentence will commence on 22 April 2006 and will expire on 21 April 2024. I decline to fix a non-parole period.

'For the murder of Sarah Kathleen Folbigg I sentence you to imprisonment for 20 years. The sentence will commence on 22 April 2013 and will expire on 21 April 2033. I decline to fix a non-parole period.

'For the murder of Laura Elizabeth Folbigg I sentence you to imprisonment for 22 years. The sentence will commence on 22 April 2021 and will expire on 21 April 2043. I fix a non-parole period of 12 years, which will expire on 21 April 2033.

'You will be eligible for parole on 21 April 2033.'

Kathleen Folbigg's father, Thomas 'Jack' Britton, had been found guilty 34 years previously for the murder of her mother, in a neighbouring courtroom to the one in which Kathy had been found guilty of killing her children. Today's proceedings had demonstrated that Jack Britton was effectively responsible for so much more than the one murder. His actions, and the abuse he had inflicted upon his daughter, had a profound influence on the outcome of her life, and the lives of her children. The abuse he had perpetrated on his daughter had impaired her capacity to develop any meaningful emotional bonds and contributed to a state of mind that led to her killing her own children.

For the murder of her four children Kathleen Folbigg had just been sentenced to 40 years in jail with a non-parole period of 30 years. She would not be able to walk free until she was at least 66 years old, well past her childbearing years. She was led from the dock. Most people in the courtroom were stunned. Craig's sister wept. Finally it was over.

Outside on the steps of the courthouse, Kathleen's solicitor, Peter Krisenthal, made an appearance before the media. 'Mrs Folbigg has asked me to say that she is innocent of these offences. She did not kill the children or harm them in any way. She has instructed me to immediately lodge an appeal against her conviction and sentence,' he said.

Kathleen's foster sister, Lea Bown, used the media spotlight to call for all sudden and unexplained infant deaths to be scrutinised more closely by police and coroners. 'It's so much easier to put down "undetermined death" when a child dies. These children have no voices. It's just inexcusable,' she said.

Meanwhile, as Kathleen was being marched to the prison van that would take her back to Silverwater her husband was contemplating a very different life sentence. For once he would not talk. Surrounded by a media scrum, he gazed fixedly into the middle distance. Perplexed by his silence, the media's questions about his impressions of the sentence quickly turned to questions about big money deals he may have stitched up with media fixers. His brother John angrily denied there had been a deal done with Harry M Miller. Craig said nothing and allowed his brother to hustle him across the busy road outside the Supreme Court of New South Wales in Sydney's Queen's Square and away to a new life, a new wife and a twilight filled with broken dreams and heartbreaking memories.

It was Detective Inspector Bernie Ryan who finally attempted to bring a note of perspective and closure to the tragic case. On the steps of the court he said: 'Spare a thought for the four lost lives. If not for certain events Caleb would have been 14 now, Patrick 13, Sarah 11 and Laura six. What would they have achieved in their lives?

'No matter what, this prosecution has always been about the Folbigg children and the search for the truth.

'May they rest in peace.'

* Kathleen Folbigg is appealing her conviction and sentence.

Acknowledgments

There are a number of very important people without whom this book would not have been published. First and foremost is Random House and its excellent non-fiction publisher Jane Southward whose vision, determination and direction made it all happen. Thanks also to my wonderful editor, Jo Butler, for all her help. I must also thank my family for their patience while this book was written and my good friends who offered encouragement and support. Notably Alison King, Angela Mollard, Nigel Wright, Barry Cronley and Sharon Mottau for listening when I needed it most. At *The Sun-Herald* I must thank Phil McLean, Peter Lynch and Liz Hannan for allowing me the time to write this book, and my colleagues Frank Walker, John Kidman, Candy Sutton, Eamonn Duff, Miranda Wood and Andrew West for their guidance and support. Special thanks must also go to Lee Glendinning for her help as the court case progressed and the lawyers who helped with my queries. I would also like to thank Detective Sergeant Bernie Ryan for doing his job so well. If it hadn't been for his investigation, there would be no book and no justice.

Photo Credits

Cover
Kathleen Folbigg: News Limited

Picture section (in order of appearance)
Caleb Folbigg: *The Sun-Herald*
Patrick Folbigg: *The Sun-Herald*
Sarah Folbigg: *The Sun-Herald*
Calendar page: *The Sun-Herald*
Laura Folbigg: News Limited
Bedroom: *The Sun-Herald*
Diary page: *The Sun-Herald*
Detective Ryan: News Limited
Newspaper article: News Limited
Thomas Britton: News Limited
Kathleen Folbigg and Tony Lambkin: News Limited
Kathleen Folbigg and Major Joyce Harmer: News Limited
Mark Tedeschi QC: Fairfax Photos
Lea Bown: News Limited
Craig Folbigg and Helen Pearce: News Limited
Craig Folbigg: News Limited
Kathleen Folbigg: News Limited